COREL DRAW
DESIGN WORKSHOP

J. SCOTT HAMLIN & BARRY MEYER

SYBEX San Francisco · Paris · Düsseldorf · Soest

Acquisitions Manager: Kristine Plachy

Developmental Editor: Melanie Spiller

Editor: Janja Lalich

Technical Editor: Deborah Maizels

Book Designer: Seventeenth Street Studios

Page layout and composition: Seventeenth Street Studios

Proofreader: Susan Burckhard

Indexer: Judy Evans

Cover Designer: Seventeenth Street Studios

Cover Illustrator: J. Scott Hamlin

Screen reproductions produced with Corel Capture.

CorelDRAW is a trademark of Corel Corporation.

SYBEX is a registered trademark of SYBEX Inc.

TRADEMARKS: SYBEX has attempted throughout this book to distinguish proprietary trademarks from descriptive terms by following the capitalization style used by the manufacturer.

Every effort has been made to supply complete and accurate information. However, SYBEX assumes no responsibility for its use, nor for any infringement of the intellectual property rights of third parties which would result from such use.

Library of Congress Card Number: 95-072477
ISBN: 0-7821-1817-8

Manufactured in the United States of America

10 9 8 7 6 5 4 3 2 1

To my wife Staci and son Aidan.
  J. Scott Hamlin

To my wife Laurie and son Jesse.
  Barry F. Meyer

Acknowledgments

J. Scott Hamlin

I'd like to thank my extraordinary wife, Staci, for supporting me through the learning and transition years, for being such an excellent wife/friend/helper, for helping me with the more tedious aspects of manuscript production, and for giving me such a wonderful son, Aidan, who provides me with much needed laughter, joy, and play breaks.

I must also thank Steve and Judy Penn, my father- and mother-in-law, for their support, and for helping us buy our first computer. I'd also like to express my appreciation to Steve Penn and Lynn Goode, for their valuable counsel.

I extend my thanks to Carrie Dopson at Corel Corporation for her timely help with my pesky requests. I am grateful for the example of technical excellence provided by Chris Dickman during my association with *The CorelDRAW Journal*. I'm indebted to Barry Meyer for providing me with useful techniques in his articles in *Corel Magazine* and *Before and After* which later became the inspiration for my own techniques. I would like to thank Melanie Spiller at Sybex for being almost as excited about this concept as we were. Her easy-going, yet quality-conscious approach made working on this book a pleasure. Finally, I'd like to express my deep gratitude to Barry Colvin and Marketing Systems Group, for allowing me to use many of the illustrations I've created for them and for giving me some breathing room to work on this book.

It is only by the grace of God that I came to be capable of doing this book. It is my hope that He be glorified by my work, since it is by His strength and grace that I was able to produce my portion of it.

Barry F. Meyer

First and foremost, I want to thank my wife and son for the love and happiness we have shared. Both have been very understanding and supportive in my obsession with computer graphics. My wife's guidance, suggestions, and help with this book have been invaluable, and my son's interest in working through my projects (and telling me when I haven't explained something well enough) has been very gratifying.

I would like to thank Ellen Adams for starting *Corel Magazine* and publishing my very first "how to" article, and Scott Campbell, the current editor of *Corel Magazine*. I wish to thank John McWade, publisher of *Before & After* magazine, for introducing me and many others to the wonders of computer illustration. I would also like to thank Corel Corporation for making a product which is accessible to the novice, powerful enough for the professional, and which has had a remarkable impact on the Windows graphics market.

I wish to thank Scott Hamlin for proposing this project in the first place, and then having the tenacity to make it happen.

Contents

Introduction

Corel has long inspired budding artists to become professional illustrators. With a large enthusiastic user base, many user groups, publications like *The CorelDRAW Journal* and *Corel Magazine,* and the annual Corel World Design Contest, CorelDRAW and other Corel programs have enjoyed a phenomenal success in the Windows graphics market. But very little published material has been dedicated to CorelDRAW illustration techniques.

This book will not attempt to teach you the CorelDRAW or Corel Photo-Paint software. Our focus is on technique, using these programs to create attractive illustrations via a project format. We assume that you either already know the fundamentals or are willing to look through the manual or help files when a question arises. Nevertheless, insights, tips, and tricks are plentiful throughout the book when relevant to the task at hand.

The techniques covered are demonstrated using version 6 of the Corel graphics suite, but many of the DRAW projects can be accomplished in any version. Corel Photo-Paint is a recent addition. With few exceptions, Corel Photo-Paint techniques can only be accomplished in version 5 or 6. When an entire project relies on a feature that is available only in a recent CorelDRAW release, you will be notified at the beginning of the project. In many cases workarounds do exist, especially for CorelDRAW techniques. For instance, the Power-Clip feature, used frequently in these projects, became available in version 5. If you're using version 3 or 4, you can usually achieve a similar effect by manually node-editing the object in question until its outline matches the outline of the PowerClip object.

Other examples are the Join With Segment option, new in version 6's Node Edit Roll-Up, and the introduction of anchor points in version 5's Transform Roll-Up. These are essentially productivity aids. If an effect can be duplicated in an earlier version, albeit with a little more effort, we consider the project appropriate for all versions.

Due to time and space limitations, we will not cover Corel Dream 3D.

Because using CorelDRAW is a visual experience, our intention is to communicate primarily through visual means. Each step is illustrated, with accompanying text for further explanation. As you become more of a Corel expert, you may find yourself looking at the next graphic and completing that step without reading the text.

Feel free to skip around to any project. Although the book follows a logical progression, each technique is fairly autonomous. Projects 1 through 8 can be seen as "fundamentals," but even the more complex projects are fully explained and can be accomplished without learning the techniques prior to it. We do strongly encourage you to read this introduction for some useful tips that will help you to accomplish all of the techniques in this book.

VISUAL CUES

Icons and other graphic elements throughout the book will help you quickly identify certain types of information.

The lightbulb icon is used to provide supplemental information, which may be background information or a more detailed explanation of a particular technique, a software-related tip or trick, or a description of variations or additional applications of the subject technique. This icon will be accompanied by the keyword *Hint, Tip,* or *Variation.*

The alarm icon, with the key word *Warning* is used to introduce additional information when some other complication might arise, such as a strain on system resources or difficulty in completing a certain task.

 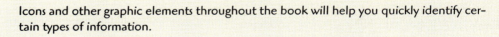

IMPORTANT NOTE: When a project is recommended for certain versions of the CorelDRAW software, an IMPORTANT NOTE can be found on the first page of the project.

CONVENTIONS

As mentioned earlier, this book assumes that you have a manual and can access help files. In the interest of clarity, we will briefly cover most of the basic CorelDRAW features and terminology that will be used throughout the projects.

Keyboard Controls, Short-cuts, and Mouse Actions

The Ctrl, Alt, and Shift Keys The abbreviation "Ctrl" stands for the Control key, "Shift" indicates the Shift key, and "Alt" refers to the Alt key. Whenever a keyboard command is used in conjunction with the + symbol, it indicates that you will need to hold both keys down at the same time, as in Ctrl+Shift. Or you can hold down one key and perform an additional mouse operation. For example, holding down the Shift key while clicking on objects or nodes to select them allows you to select more than one object or node at a time. This operation is referred to as Shift+select.

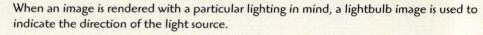

When an image is rendered with a particular lighting in mind, a lightbulb image is used to indicate the direction of the light source.

In order to help you focus on the particular object being created or manipulated, that object is shown in full color or a bold line weight. Previously created objects, or sections that are not being manipulated, are shown in gray or in a finer line weight for reference.

Marquee/Marquee-select Since we are not sure if "marquee" has officially become a verb, we will refer to selecting objects or nodes with a marquee as marquee-selecting. You can hold down the Shift key while marquee-selecting to add objects or nodes to the current selection, referred to as "Shift+marquee-select."

Blue dashed lines represent CorelDRAW's guidelines.

Color designations

When applicable, a list of colors is given at the beginning of a project. You can create a palette of these colors or enter the color values in the fill dialog box each time the color is used. Color mixes are given as a percentage followed by a letter representing the process color. For example, a red composed of 100% magenta and 100% yellow is described as 100%M, 100%Y.

Menu selections

Menu and dialog box references are punctuated and capitalized as they appear in the program. A progression through menu options is indicated by a right pointing arrow, as in Effects ➢ PowerClip ➢ Place Inside Container.

WHAT'S NEW IN CORELDRAW 6

This list is by no means comprehensive, but rather an indication of those new features that are relevant to the projects in this book.

User-Defined Interface

Both CorelDRAW 6 and Corel Photo-Paint 6 have customizable interfaces that allow tremendous control over how the interfaces interact with these programs. Accessed via Tools ➢ Customize, there are five tab choices:

- ■ Keyboard: assigns shortcut keys to all Menu, Roll-Up, and Toolbox items

- Menu: relocates Menu items
- Toolbars: places buttons for all Menu and Toolbox items along the Toolbar near the top of the screen or in the Toolbox at the left of the screen (their default locations)
- Roll-Ups: relocates Roll-Up items to different Roll-Up groups
- Color Palette: modifies color palette options

Typically, we will refer to a particular action by its Tool or Menu name, without stating its default location or shortcut key. There are occasional exceptions, particularly if we think the action we're referring to is not commonly used, or if it's buried inside a series of menus. In those cases, we will refer to the default menu path or the shortcut keys.

The Shaping Operations—Intersection, Weld, and Trim

As a wonderful aid to object creation, CorelDRAW 4 introduced the Weld operation, and version 5 added the Intersection and Trim operations. In these earlier versions, you selected the objects you wanted and clicked the Intersection, Weld, or Trim menu item. Selecting Weld connected all the objects selected into one continuous curve, removing any overlap. The original objects were deleted. The Intersection operation creates a new object outlining only the overlap of the selected objects. All the originally selected objects remained. The Trim operation removed the overlap from one of the selected objects leaving the remaining object(s) intact. The object trimmed was either the last object selected or, for a marquee-select, the bottom object in the stacking order.

DRAW 6 added several options to these basic shaping operations and increased the complexity of using them. If you select Intersection, Weld, or Trim from the Arrange menu, the Shaping Roll-Up Group appears, and the menu option you selected becomes the active page. Each page has checkbox options to Leave Original Target Object or Leave Original Other Object(s). In addition, depending on which operation is active, there is a button at the bottom of the Roll-Up labeled Intersect With, Weld To, or Trim. To use these operations, select one or more objects, check the appropriate boxes, click the button at the bottom of the Roll-Up, and then click one additional object on screen. The chosen operation is performed as described above, and the last object selected remains intact if Leave Original Target Object is selected. The original object(s) selected remains if Leave Original Other Object(s) is selected. (In version 5, to leave any of the original objects intact, first duplicate them and then perform the operation on the duplicates. Alternatively, you could copy the objects to the clipboard, perform the operation on the originals, and paste the copies back in.)

You can also customize DRAW 6 by adding variations of the Intersection, Weld, and Trim operations to any menu using Tools ➢ Customize ➢ Menu. Three of these—Quick Intersect, Quick Weld, and Quick Trim—behave the same as the original Intersection, Weld, and Trim operations in DRAW 5. The other three—Intersect With, Weld To, and Trim Object—allow you to select one or more objects, click the menu option, and select one more object to perform that operation.

DRAW 6 allows you to use the shaping operations in many different ways. Unless there is a particularly complicated series of steps that must be performed in a precise way, we have used the generic description of Intersect, Weld, or Trim. Feel free to use your favorite approach to accomplish the task.

Join With Segment/Extend Curve to Close

DRAW 6's Node Edit Roll-Up has a new tool that automatically joins two end nodes of a curve with a straight line. In previous versions, you connected the nodes by drawing a line, combining the objects, marquee-selecting any unjoined nodes, and clicking the Join Nodes button in the Node Edit Roll-Up. Corel 6 has called this feature "Join With Segment" in the Node Editing folder of the Keyboard and Menu tabs in the Customize dialog box, "Extend Curve to Close" in the Node Editing folder in the Toolbars tab (with the mouse pointer over this button), and "Extend button" in the DRAW Help Index under "nodes, adding, connecting." We refer to this feature as Join With Segment.

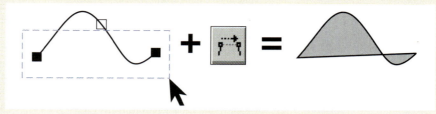

To use the Join With Segment feature, select two end nodes of an object, and click the button. The nodes are joined with a straight line, and the object is closed. (See the example above.) A fill could then be applied if desired. Since you must have both of the nodes selected at the same time, it is necessary that the nodes to be joined are part of the same object. In DRAW's terminology, two separate curve segments can be part of one object. Just select the two, and choose Arrange ➣ Combine.

The Knife Tool

The Knife Tool is located in the Shape Tool flyout. To access the Knife Tool, press and hold the Shape Tool button in the Toolbox or click the triangle in the lower-right corner of the Shape Tool button. A flyout appears with buttons for the Shape Tool, Knife Tool, and Eraser Tool. Slide the mouse cursor over the Knife Tool, and release. The Knife Tool button replaces the Shape Tool in the Toolbox.

In previous DRAW versions, you cut an object by first selecting it with the Shape Tool, clicking on the object where you wanted it cut, and clicking the Break Curve button in the Node Edit Roll-Up. If you wanted to individually edit the cut segments, you chose Break Apart in the Arrange menu. This method is still available to version 6 users. Coauthor Scott frequently prefers this method (he finds it easier to control) so you'll be seeing it a lot in his projects.

The Knife Tool has options that can duplicate, and go beyond, the functionality of the Break Curve feature. Double-click the Knife Tool and the Tool Properties dialog appears, with Knife preselected in the Tools drop-down menu. In the General tab, there are checkboxes for Leave as one object and Automatically close object. With neither of these selected, knifing an object creates two separate objects. Each object can be edited individually, and the result is functionally the same as using the Break Curve and Break Apart options. When Leave as one object is checked, the Knife Tool cuts the curve, but it remains as one object. If this sounds confusing, it's like clicking the Break Curve button in the Node Edit Roll-Up but not selecting Break Apart. Since the object is cut, it cannot be filled, but edits (such as changing the line weight) are applied to the entire object. If Automatically close object is checked, an object knifed in half will result in each piece being automatically closed with a straight line, to which a fill can be applied.

To use the Knife Tool, position it over the curve section you want to cut. It will change from slanted to vertical when it is properly positioned and available for use. Then click the left mouse button.

The Polygon Tool

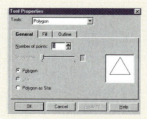

The Polygon tool provides an easy way to create polygons. The Polygon Properties Sheet, accessed by double-clicking on the Polygon Tool, allows you to create many kinds of polygons by changing the number of sides, and by selecting the Star or Polygon as Star options. Corel has also introduced mirror editing with this feature, which allows you to maintain the symmetry of a polygon by moving respective nodes in conjunction with one another. Although there are plenty of possibilities with the Polygon Tool, we will mainly use its ability to render triangles easily.

WHAT'S NEW IN COREL PHOTO-PAINT 6

Corel Photo-Paint has been transformed into a full-featured image-editing program in version 6. Here, we approach it as a support program for CorelDRAW. You can access Corel Photo-Paint from within DRAW by clicking on the Application Launcher button.

Large file Capacity

Corel Photo-Paint 5 and 5 Plus were limited to 16-megabyte file sizes. With Corel Photo-Paint 6, you are limited only by your computer's resources.

Alpha Channels Support

Corel Photo-Paint 5 introduced transparency masks that were not compatible with the industry-standard alpha channels. Version 6 offers complete alpha channel support, and refers to alpha channels simply as channels. A channel is a mask that uses grayscale values to regulate the degree to which an effect is applied to a given image. The lighter the grayscale value, the more an effect is applied. A basic mask is a channel that has two values: black and white. An effect is applied where the value is white, and not applied where the value is black. In version 6, there is no real difference between a mask and a channel. Any file that Corel Photo-Paint can open can be used as a channel. All images are converted to grayscale when opened as channels. All techniques demonstrated in this book using channels can be easily duplicated using transparency masks in versions 5 and 5 Plus.

OUR FAVORITE TECHNIQUES

Creating Duplicates

CorelDRAW has an incredible number of ways to create duplicates of objects. Some of the methods frequently used in this book are outlined here.

- The Duplicate command places a duplicate of an object at a distance from the original as specified in Options ➢ General ➢ Place duplicates and clones.
- The Plus [+] key on the numeric keypad always places a duplicate directly on top of the original.
- As you drag an object, click the right mouse button to leave the original behind and drop the duplicate in a new location. This also works when using the mouse to transform an object (i.e., scale, skew, or rotate).
- You can Copy and Paste an object. DRAW will paste an object in its original location, handy if you want a copy of an object but want it temporarily out of the way so you can edit the original. Just don't copy anything else in the meantime, or it will replace the previously copied object on the Clipboard.
- The Transform Roll-Up lets you apply the transformation to a duplicate (using the Apply To Duplicate button), leaving the original object intact.
- In the Layers Roll-Up, you can copy an object to another layer by pressing the right-pointing triangle and clicking Copy To, and selecting a new layer.

Note that a clone is different from a duplicate. If you create a clone of an object and edit the original, the clone will also be altered.

PowerClip

The PowerClip feature was a version 5.0 addition. An object that is PowerClipped into another object will be visible only within the boundaries of the second object. In DRAW's vernacular, the objects clipped inside are called the contents, and the clipping object is called the container. The PowerClip feature has four separate options: Place Inside Container, Extract Contents, Edit Contents, and Finish Editing This Level.

To use the PowerClip feature, select an object, choose Place Inside Container, and click on the desired container object. To edit objects that have already been PowerClipped, choose Edit Contents. If the Wireframe preview mode is not selected, the contents will appear in full color, and the container will be shown with a blue outline only. Make any changes to the contents, and choose Finish Editing This Level to return DRAW to its normal editing mode. You can also "nest" PowerClips (which means to place contents into a container which is itself already a content object). To edit nested PowerClips, choose Edit Contents repeatedly until the desired content's objects are visible. Make your changes, and choose Finish Editing This Level the appropriate number of times to back out to DRAW's normal editing mode. If you want to remove contents from a PowerClip container, choose Extract Contents.

Sometimes the objects you want to place inside a container completely obscure that container, making it difficult or impossible to select. If the contents and container objects reside on the same layer, select the content's objects and press Shift+PgDn (To Back). The contents will still be selected and the screen will redraw with the desired container object in front. Choose Place Inside Container, and click on the container object.

One more thing about PowerClips. In Tool ➤ Options ➤ General, there's a checkbox labeled "Automatically center new powerclip contents." (In DRAW 5, it's Special ➤ Preferences ➤ General ➤ Auto-Center Place Inside.) To demonstrate, example A shows a circle overlapping a square. Example B illustrates where the circle ends up when the PowerClip feature is used with the Automatically center new powerclip contents option turned on. Example C illustrates where the circle is placed when you use the PowerClip feature with the Automatically center new powerclip contents option turned off. If the Automatically center new powerclip contents feature turned off and the object you are going to PowerClip is outside of the intended container, as in example D, the result will be similar to example E.

Corel was concerned that the novice user might accidentally PowerClip an object into a container that it didn't overlap, appearing like the effect did not work. So Corel created this option, which is turned on by default. We suggest that the experienced user turn this feature off.

Blend

It's beyond the scope of this introduction to describe all of the options DRAW offers when blending two objects, but some of our favorites are the abilities to blend objects along a path, to map nodes, and to blend grouped objects. These variations are described in detail when used in the projects. We do want to discuss the ability to set the number of Blend steps, and the effect this has on the final output of your DRAW file. Sometimes we use the Blend effect to create a discernible number of intermediate blend objects. Usually we've used the Blend effect to create a smooth transition between two colors. Here are the steps you'll need:

First, take the greatest percentage change in the Cyan, Magenta, Yellow, or Black components of the two blend objects. Multiply that value by 2.56. Then, take the distance that the blend covers in inches or parts of an inch. Multiply that by 150. (This assumes a 150-lpi output typical for high-quality printing. If your output is intended for a different line resolution, then use that value.) The number of Blend steps is the lesser of the two values. For example, if you're blending between a red object (100%M, 100%Y) and a yellow object (20%M, 100%Y), over a distance of .75 inches, the greatest color change is 80%M. Multiply by 2.56 to get 204. But .75 times 150 is only 112. So, 112 steps is the value to use. If the blend distance were increased to 2 inches (2 x 150 = 300), the 204 value would be used.

Two other Blend concerns should be mentioned. The first occurs when a blend is spread over too large a distance. If you specify a 5% black change over an entire page width, the maximum number of shades available is 13 (.05 times 256). Thirteen shades in a 8.5-inch area will almost certainly be noticeable.

Another concern is whether to blend filled shapes or lines to get smooth gradations. We prefer to blend shapes whenever possible, for one reason. If you don't use enough Blend steps for the line weight used, you may have gaps where the background shows through. Sometimes these aren't visible on a normal preview (although they should be when zoomed way in) and show up only on output. Also, if the graphic is later resized and the line weight isn't set to scale with it, you will have the same problem.

Transform Functions

The transform functions include the ability to position, rotate, scale and mirror, size, and skew objects. DRAW allows you to do this through dialog boxes or mouse actions. The Transform Roll-Up group is accessed via Arrange ➤ Transform ➤ [appropriate submenu]. Selecting either Position (Alt+F8), Rotate (Alt+F9), Scale and Mirror (Alt+F9), Size (Alt+F10) or Skew (Alt+F11) will open the Transform Roll-Up with the specific selected page active. The shortcut keys are listed because we frequently find them convenient.

The Rotate, Scale and Mirror, and Skew functions warrant further discussion. These three options allow the selection of any one of nine anchor points. An anchor point is a point relative to the object's highlighting box that will not move. The anchor point choices are located at the corners, midway along the sides, and at the center of the object's highlighting box. The selected operation modifies the object relative to that point. This option is accessed by clicking the downward-pointing triangle in the lower-right corner of the Roll-Up.

You can also rotate, scale and mirror, and skew objects using the mouse. Select an object and eight handles (squares) appear around the circumference of the object. Dragging any one of the corner handles scales the object proportionately. Dragging any one of the middle-side handles scales the object horizontally or vertically, which DRAW calls stretching. Pressing the Shift key while dragging scales relative to the center of the object. Pressing the Ctrl key while dragging scales the object in 100% increments, a handy way to mirror an object. As you drag past the boundary of the object, it snaps to an exact mirror image.

If you double-click an object, or click again on an already-selected object, the rotate and skew handles appear. The rotate handles are curved, double-headed arrows at the corners of the object. The skew handles are straight, double-headed arrows midway along the sides of the object. These handles work predictably, dragging a rotate handle rotates the object, and dragging a skew handle skews the object. In addition, when the rotate and skew handles are active, the center-of-rotation marker is also visible. This marker is a circle with a dot in it, and its default position is in the center of the object. You can drag it anywhere you like; and with Snap To Objects turned on, you can snap it to any of the object's nodes (or any other object for that matter). Other snap modes work as well. Dragging a rotate handle rotates the object around that point.

When using the mouse to transform an object, the amount of transformation is shown in the Status Bar.

A highlighting box is an imaginary rectangle which bounds the farthest extent of an object's nodes, or control points. DRAW's use of nodes and control points to determine the boundary of an object (as opposed to the farthest extent of the object's outline) causes several problems. If you ever have trouble snapping an object's outline to a guide-line, marquee-selecting an object, or encountering many of numerous other seemingly inexplicable problems, this highlighting box anomaly may be the reason.

Fountain-fill Options

DRAW 6 has a mind-boggling number of options for applying fountain fills. These include four different types: Linear, Radial, Conical, and Square. Depending on the type selected, you have the ability to set the angle and center position of the effect. You can specify multiple colors for fountain fills, and set edge-pad values. We refer you to Corel's documentation and Help files to learn how to utilize the various fountain-fill options to their full capability, but certain aspects warrant discussion here.

The first thing we need to explain is the way DRAW spans a fountain fill across an object. DRAW places the range of colors specified across the entire highlighting box of the object, then clips the colors displayed into the object's outline. It's as if you drew a rectangle coinciding with the highlighting box of an object, then PowerClipped that rectangle into the object. (And remember, DRAW bases the highlighting box on the farthest extent of the nodes *and* control points, so the box can be quite a bit larger than the outline of the object.) DRAW allows the user to specify Edge-pad values which pad the edge of the fountain fill with solid areas of the specified From and To colors. If you want to fill an object with a fountain fill from black to white, for example, and the highlighting box is larger than the object, you would have to "play" with the Edge-pad values to get the desired result.

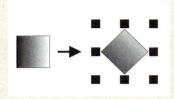

This really gets complicated when rotating an object. Let's say you've carefully adjusted the Edge-pad values to get the exact effect you're looking for. When you rotate the object, the highlighting box does not rotate, but rather expands or contracts to fit the object's new orientation altering the way the fountain fill spans the object. For a demonstration, draw a square and fill it with a 0 degree Two Color Linear Fountain Fill: From: Black; To: White. The fill spans the square from black to white, which is expected since the highlighting box coincides with the circumference of the square. Now rotate the square 45 degrees. Look at the handles and you'll see that the highlighting box has expanded. The fountain fill in the rotated square now blends from about 75%K to about 25%K. (A workaround to this is to export the unrotated object in encapsulated PostScript or Adobe Illustrator format. This converts the fountain fills to incrementally-colored basic shapes, which can be imported back in using the interpreted PostScript or Adobe Illustrator filter. When rotated, these images will not alter their appearance.)

Another concern is DRAW's Custom Fountain Fills, which allow you to assign multiple colors to any of the fountain-fill types. If you assign many different colors, the final output could be banded. DRAW has historically limited the output of fountain fills to 256 colors. If you've assigned a Two Color Fountain Fill, 256 shades is plenty to smoothly gradate from the one color to the other. But let's say you've assigned a Custom Fountain Fill which alternates back and forth ten times between black and white. Each band of black to white only has 25 colors available to render that blend (assuming equal spacing for all the custom colors). This is not enough for a smooth gradation, and banding would most likely be visible. DRAW 5 partially addressed this by allowing up to 2000 fountain steps to be assigned when printing directly from DRAW to a Postscript printer (File ➢ Print ➢ Options ➢ Options ➢ Fountain Steps). DRAW 6 has expanded this solution by adding Auto increase fountain steps, Optimize fountain fills, and Banded fountain fill warnings to the Postscript Print options.

These can be found in File ➢ Print ➢ Options ➢ Options ➢ PostScript Preferences.

Auto increase fountain steps increases the number of steps used to render the fill so that banding will not occur. Optimize fountain fills reduces the number of steps in fills that have more than the necessary number to render a smooth gradation. Banded fountain fill warnings displays a warning if a Linear Fountain Fill is likely to show banding when printed.

Equally important, you can now specify increased Fountain steps to a maximum of 2000, and auto increase fountain steps can be selected, in the EPS Export dialog box.

(Note: The fountain steps we've been discussing are not to be confused with the Preview fountain steps option in Tools ➢ Options ➢ Display, which controls only the number of steps used to display a fountain fill on your monitor.)

Nudge

We are very fond of DRAW's Nudge feature. You can use the arrow keys to move an object or nodes a specified distance, by adjusting the setting in Tools ➢ Options ➢ Nudge. Set Nudge to a very small value to carefully position objects or nodes. Set Nudge to a larger value to repeatedly move objects a consistent distance.

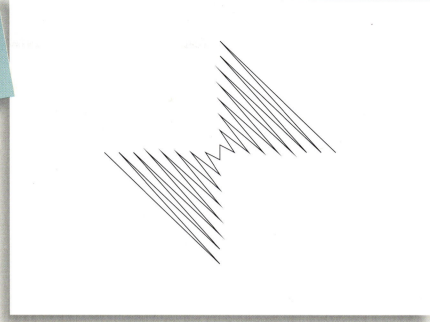

Reviewing the Basics of Lines

What you will learn

- Drawing a jagged line
- Manipulating a jagged line
- Rotating and stretching nodes
- Drawing curved lines
- Nudging Beziér control points
- Breaking apart and joining nodes

orelDRAW deals with lines in both a simple and complex manner. In CorelDRAW, lines are defined by nodes. Mastering nodes will give you complete control over lines and shapes. Nodes can be manipulated using either the Shape Tool, the Node Edit dialog box, or keyboard shortcuts. Before you can manipulate nodes, however, you need a line.

Drawing a Jagged Line

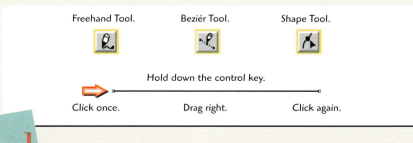

Freehand Tool.   Beziér Tool.   Shape Tool.

Hold down the control key.

Click once.   Drag right.   Click again.

Draw a straight line by selecting the Freehand Tool. Hold down the Ctrl key and click the left mouse button once. Move the mouse to the right, and click the left button again. To add nodes to a line, open the Node Edit dialog box.

2 Select the Shape Tool (second tool from the top in the toolbar). Click on the line. Marquee-select both nodes. Click four times on the Plus (+) button in the Node Edit dialog box. Fifteen evenly spaced nodes will be added to the line.

3 You can select nodes by marquee-selecting them or by clicking on them. Holding down the Shift key while selecting nodes (Shift+select) with the Shape Tool allows you to select more than one node.

Drag down.

Starting with the first node on the left, Shift+select every other node with the Shape Tool. Ctrl+drag the nodes down about half an inch.

If you click on a node and accidentally move it, select Undo. The move will be canceled, but the node will still be selected.

HINT

Here are some quick ways to open the Node Edit Roll-Up. The keyboard shortcut is Ctrl+F10. You can also double-click on the Shape Tool, a line segment, or a node.

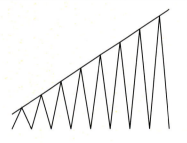

Manipulating a Jagged Line

1 Lines can be used as guidelines with the Snap To Objects feature. Draw a straight line. Press Ctrl+D to duplicate it once. Choose Tools ➤ Options dialog box. Set Place duplicates and clones to Horizontal 0 inches and Vertical –2 inches. With the Shape Tool, select the right node on the original line. Ctrl+drag the node up about 1.75 inches. Select the Shape Tool. Click on the original line. Marquee-select both

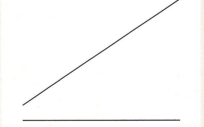

nodes. Click four times on the Plus (+) button in the Node Edit dialog box to add 15 evenly spaced nodes to the line. Repeat this process for the bottom duplicate line.

2 In the Layout menu, check the Snap To Object option. Select the second node from the left on the duplicate line. Ctrl+drag the node upward until it snaps to its corresponding node on the diagonal line. Repeat this process with every other node.

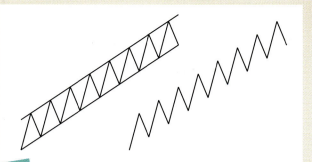

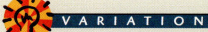

VARIATION

This technique can be used with just about any line shape, such as the curved lines shown here.

3 With the Pick Tool, select the diagonal line. Ctrl+drag downward about half an inch, and click the right mouse button. With the Shape Tool, select the node on the far left of the jagged line. Drag it down to the corresponding node on the lower diagonal line. Repeat this process for every other node, dragging upward when the corresponding nodes on the lower diagonal line are above those on the jagged line. Delete the two diagonal lines when you are finished.

Rotating Nodes

Nodes can also be rotated. Create another line. Marquee-select both nodes. Click five times on the Plus (+) button in the Node Edit dialog box. Thirty evenly spaced nodes will be added to the line. Starting with the second node on the left, Shift+select every other node with the Shape Tool. Select the Rotate button in the Node Edit dialog box. Hold down the Ctrl key, and rotate the nodes 90 degrees.

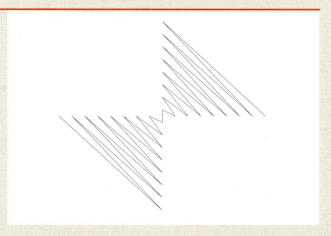

Stretching Nodes

1 Nodes can be stretched. Create another line and duplicate it four times, each line about .25 inches from the last. Combine the lines by marquee-ing all the lines with the Pick Tool, then selecting Combine from the Arrange menu. Select all of the nodes by marqueeing them with the Shape Tool. Click two times on the Plus (+) button in the Node Edit dialog box to add three nodes to each line. Shift+marquee-select the second and fourth sets of nodes.

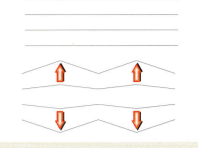

Select the Stretch button in the Node Edit dialog box. Shift+select the bottom-middle control bar. Stretch the nodes by dragging downward until the Status Bar reads about 175 degrees.

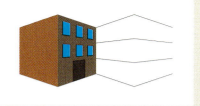

Here's an example of how these lines can be used as perspective guides.

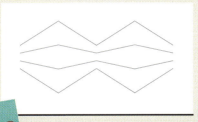

2 The left and right center sets of nodes can be stretched to deepen the perspective lines . . .

3 . . . Or you can rotate the center set of nodes 180 degrees to push the perspective lines to the vanishing point . . .

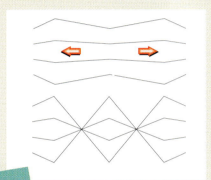

4 . . . Or you can push the second and third sets of nodes to the left and right respectively, and then rotate the center set of nodes to widen the middle.

Drawing Curved Lines

1 With this technique, you can create curved or wavy lines. Draw two lines approximately 1 inch apart. Combine them. Select all of the nodes with the Shape Tool. Click three times on the Plus (+) button in the Node Edit dialog box. With all

of the nodes selected, click on the Convert To Curves icon in the Node Edit dialog box. Shift+select every other pair of nodes. Click on the Stretch button in the Node Edit dialog box. Select the bottom-center control box, and drag it downward (to scale it) about 150%.

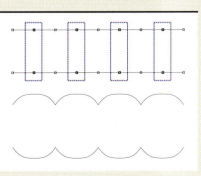

2 Using Break Apart from the Arrange menu, break apart the two lines. Delete the top one.

3 Experimenting with the Stretch and Rotate tools in the Node Edit dialog box can yield attractive and useful results. These two samples were created using multiple combinations of the node Stretch and Rotate techniques.

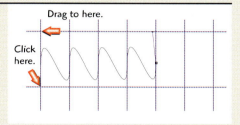

VARIATION

Beziér control points can be made to snap to guidelines and to other nodes. Place seven guidelines .5 inches apart horizontally, and two guidelines 1 inch apart vertically. In the Layout menu, turn on Snap To Guidelines. Select the Beziér Tool. Click at the intersection of the bottom leftmost guidelines, and repeat every .5 inches. This technique can be duplicated using Grids.

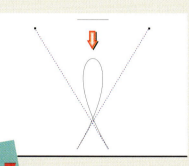

Drag to here.

Click here.

Nudging Beziér Control Points

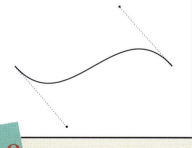

Nudge down.

1 Another way to create smooth curved lines is to take advantage of the fact that Beziér control points can be nudged. Draw a straight line. Convert it to curves by selecting the nodes with the Shape Tool, and then clicking on the Convert To Curves icon in the Node Edit Roll-Up. Select the left node with the Shape Tool, then select its adjoining Beziér control point.

If you inadvertently move the control point while selecting it, you can cancel the move by selecting Undo.

2 Make sure your nudge setting is set to .100 inches in the Options dialog box. Press the down button on your keyboard ten times. Repeat this process on the right node's Beziér control point, nudging up instead of down.

3 You can create this loop from a small line segment. Convert the line to curves. Then nudge the Beziér curves equal distances in opposite directions.

Breaking Apart Nodes

Breaking apart and joining nodes are among the most fundamental and essential technical skills needed in order to accomplish many of the techniques described in this book. While these skills may seem easy and basic, they are critical. To avoid any confusion, let's take a quick look at how to accomplish these important tasks. First, breaking apart nodes.

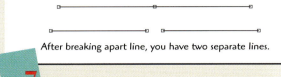

1 Draw a straight, 2-inch horizontal line. Open the Node Edit Roll-Up, and select the Shape Tool. Select the line. Marquee-select both nodes. Add a single node to the line by clicking on the Add Node button in the Node Edit Roll-Up.

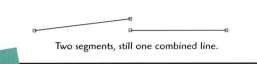

Two segments, still one combined line.

2 Note that the Status Bar indicates that there are three nodes. Select the center node. Choose the Break Node button from the Node Edit dialog box. At this point, you will have two nodes occupying the same space where previously there was only one. The Status Bar should now indicate that there are four nodes on the line. If you select one of the center nodes and drag it up, you will see that the line is now made of two combined line segments. You have broken apart the node, but the line is still combined.

After breaking apart line, you have two separate lines.

3 If you've moved one of the center nodes, select Undo to reposition it. Select Arrange ➢ Break Apart to break apart the two line segments. At this point, you will have two lines, each made up of two nodes.

When you are asked to break apart a node, unless otherwise noted, you must break apart the node *and* the line segments.

Joining Nodes

Combine lines.

1 Obviously, joining nodes is the reverse of breaking them apart. Nodes cannot be joined unless the lines are combined into one line. Marquee-select both of the lines you just broke apart. Select Arrange ➢ Combine.

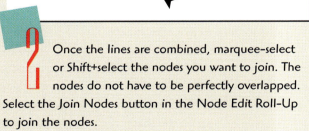

2 Once the lines are combined, marquee-select or Shift+select the nodes you want to join. The nodes do not have to be perfectly overlapped. Select the Join Nodes button in the Node Edit Roll-Up to join the nodes.

When you are asked to join nodes, you must both combine the lines and join the nodes.

Using the Shape Tools to Make Lines

What you will learn

- Drawing waves
- Creating basic spirals
- Creating variable spirals and dwindling spirals
- Rendering spiral ribbons and intertwining spiral ribbons
- Positioning objects with spirals
- Creating curved arrows
- Creating flags
- Creating lines from squares

Drawing Waves

Select the Ellipse Tool. Draw a perfect circle by holding down the Ctrl key. Make the circle about 1 inch in diameter. With the circle still selected, convert it to curves by selecting Convert To Curves from the Arrange menu, or by pressing Ctrl+Q. Double-click on the Shape Tool to open the Node Edit Roll-Up. Select the Shape Tool. With the tool, select the bottom and left nodes. Break apart the nodes by selecting the Break Node button in the Node Edit Roll-Up. Now select Break Apart from the Arrange menu, or press Ctrl+K.

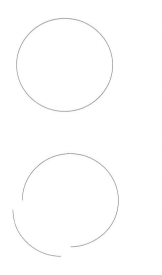

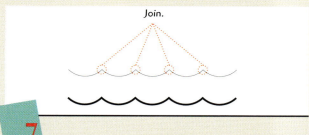

Join.

2

Delete the larger circle segment. Double-click on the remaining segment with the Pick Tool. Click on one of the rotation handles, and rotate the segment 45 degrees while holding down on the Control key to constrain the rotation to increments of 15 degrees.

3

In Tools ➢ Options dialog box, set Place duplicates and clones to Horizontal -1 inch and Vertical 0 inches. Duplicate the wave four times. Select all of the segments. Click on Combine from the Arrange menu, or press Ctrl+L. Join each segment by marquee-selecting overlapping nodes with the Node Edit tool, and selecting the Join Nodes button in the Node Edit Roll-Up.

VARIATION

To make waves that crest higher, use half-circles and repeat the previous steps.

By mirroring or inverting every other segment, you can create squiggles.

Plenty of other things can be rendered with circle segments, such as this umbrella and canoe.

Creating Basic Spirals

While CorelDRAW 6 has a new concentric spiral tool, the spirals it creates are not quite as precise or smooth as those created with circles. The following method for creating spirals with circles also has some variations that are not possible with the new spiral tool.

1 Draw a 2-inch circle. Convert To Curves. Open the Transform Roll-Up. Click on the Scale and Mirror button. Enter 10% for both Horizontal and Vertical scales. Click on Apply To Duplicate.

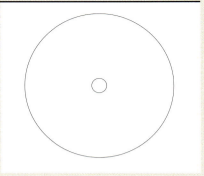

2 Select both circles. Blend with 20 steps. (The 20 Blend steps are for the purpose of this example only. Once you've mastered this technique, use as many steps as you need.) Separate, Ungroup, and Combine all of the resulting circles using the commands on the Arrange menu.

3 With the Shape Tool, marquee-select all of the horizontal nodes. Break them apart by selecting the Break Node button in the Node Edit Roll-Up. Now select Break Apart from the Arrange menu.

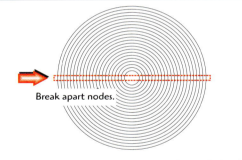

Break apart nodes.

4 Marquee-select all of the top half-circles. Combine them. Make sure that the Snap To Objects option is on. Click on the newly combined semicircle segments with the Shape Tool. Marquee-select all of the nodes. Ctrl+drag them to the left so that the outermost line snaps to the next node on the left.

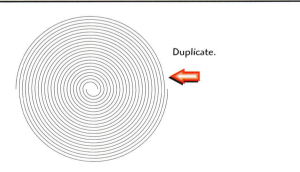

Duplicate.

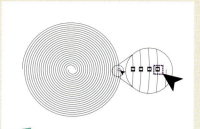

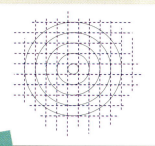

5 Combine all the segments. Join all the nodes individually where they connect. You may need to zoom in closer in order to marquee-select the overlapping nodes before joining them.

6 You now have two spirals. Press Ctrl+K to break them apart. Delete one of the spirals.

7 If you want the spiral's curves to be equal distance apart, build a grid with Guidelines, or use the Grid feature. For example, the grid here was created by placing guidelines every .25 inches. Then, using the Snap To Guidelines option, the circles were drawn equal distance apart.

8 When the half-circle segments are moved, the result is yet another kind of spiral.

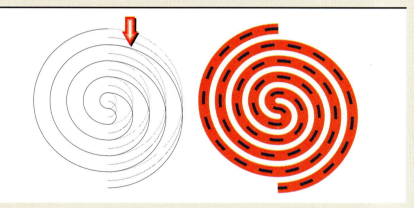

VARIATION
Experiment with different Blend steps and Outline settings to achieve the perfect spirals for your design.

Creating Variable Spirals

1 Begin by placing two vertical guidelines 3 inches apart, and two horizontal guidelines 1 inch apart. Place another horizontal guideline .375 inches above the lower guideline. The most accurate way to position guidelines is by using the Guidelines Setup dialog box located in the Layout menu. With Snap To Guidelines on, within the guidelines, draw a 1-inch-high by 3-inch-wide oval. Convert To Curves.

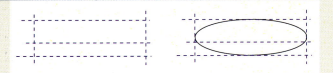

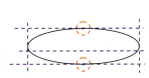

2 Open the Node Edit Roll-Up (Ctrl+F10). With the Shape Tool, select the top-middle and bottom-middle nodes. Click on the Break Node button in the Node Edit Roll-Up. Press Ctrl+K to break apart all of the nodes. You now have two ellipse segments—one on the left and another on the right.

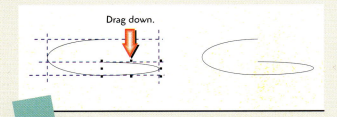

Drag down.

3 Select the ellipse segment on the right. Drag the top-middle bounding box down to the .375-inch guideline. Shift+select the two ellipse segments. Combine. With the Shape Tool, marquee-select the two nodes where the combined segments meet. Click on the Join Nodes button in the Node Edit Roll-Up. When you select an object with the Shape Tool, nodes that are on top of each other appear darker than the other nodes.

4 In Tools ➤ Options, set Place duplicates and clones to Horizontal 0 inches and Vertical –.625 inches. Select the original segment. Press Ctrl+D to duplicate it several times. Combine all the segments. Join the nodes where the segments connect.

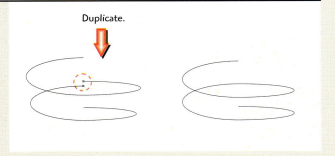

Duplicate.

Nodes can be either added or broken apart at existing junctions to manipulate the spiral as needed.

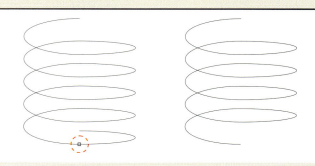

VARIATION

Any number of variations can be achieved by using different-sized ellipses.

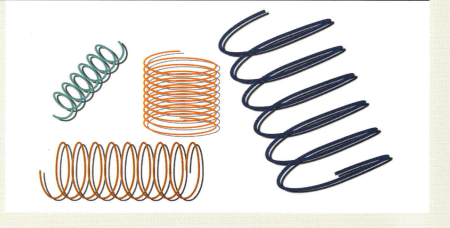

Creating Dwindling Spirals

A useful variation on the technique used to render spirals can also be useful for creating dwindling spirals.

Select the segment in step 3 of the above spiral technique. Select Arrange ➢ Transform Roll-Up. Choose the Scale and Mirror button (Alt+F9). Set both Horizontal and Vertical scales to 30% (a random percentage for illustration purposes only). Click on Apply To Duplicate. Ctrl+drag the new, smaller curve down a few inches.

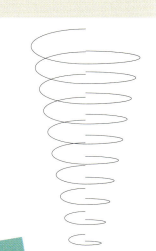

Select both elements. Blend with nine steps. (Again, this is a random number. You may use any number of steps you wish.) Separate and Ungroup the resulting blend.

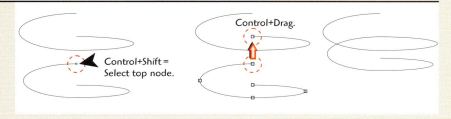

Control+Drag.

Control+Shift =
Select top node.

3 Here's a very useful trick to drag each segment into position. Make sure that the Snap To Objects option is on in the Layout menu. While holding down the Ctrl and Shift keys, click on the top node on the next spiral segment. Release the Shift key. Ctrl+drag the segment to the node on the original spiral segment, as

shown. Depending on how many steps you add, you may need to drag up or down.

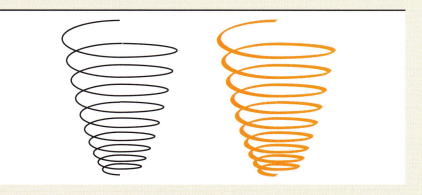

4 Repeat this technique with each segment.
Experimenting with different outline characteristics can yield attractive results with these spirals. The right spiral above utilizes the Stretch and Angle functions in the Outline Pen dialog box to achieve a calligraphic effect.

Rendering Spiral Ribbons

1 Draw an ellipse 3 inches wide and 1 inch high.
Convert the ellipse to curves. Choose Arrange ➢ Break Apart to break apart the nodes on the right and left as indicated. Delete the top half of the ellipse.

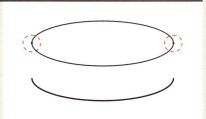

2 Break apart the center node. Mirror the left ellipse segment downward. To mirror the segment, click on it with the selection tool, select the top-middle bounding box, and Ctrl+drag the segment downward until it flips downward.

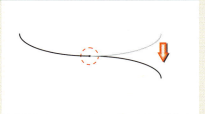

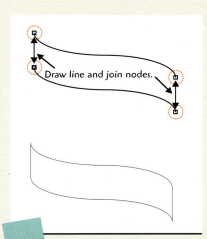

Draw line and join nodes.

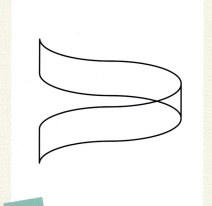

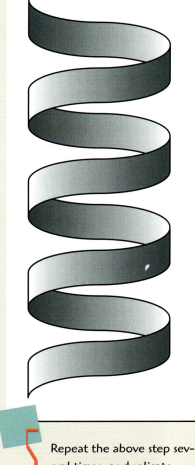

3 In Options, set Place duplicates and clones to Horizontal 0 inches and Vertical .75 inches. Shift+select the two nodes, and select Combine from the Arrange menu (Ctrl+L). Open the Node Edit Roll-Up. Marquee-select the two right corresponding nodes. Click on the top-right button (Join With Segments button) in the Node Edit Roll-Up. Repeat this process with the two corresponding nodes.

4 In Options, set Place duplicates and clones to Horizontal 0 inches and Vertical -1 inch. Duplicate the ribbon segment. Open the Transform Roll-Up. Select the Scale and Mirror button. Click on the Horizontal Mirror button. Click on the Apply button.

5 Repeat the above step several times, or duplicate each segment several times with Place duplicates and clones set to Horizontal 0 inches and Vertical -2 inches. Fill each ribbon segment with gradient fills, as shown here.

Rendering Intertwining Spiral Ribbons

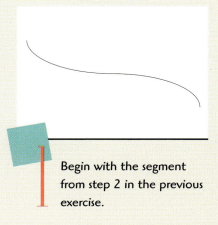

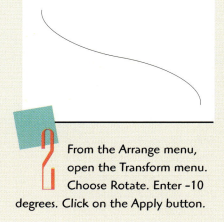

1 Begin with the segment from step 2 in the previous exercise.

2 From the Arrange menu, open the Transform menu. Choose Rotate. Enter -10 degrees. Click on the Apply button.

  PROJECT **2** USING THE SHAPE TOOLS TO MAKE LINES

3 In Options, set Place duplicates and clones to Horizontal 0 inches and Vertical .75 inches. Shift+select the two nodes, and select Combine from the Arrange menu (Ctrl+L). Open the Node Edit Roll-Up. Marquee-select the two right corresponding nodes. Click on the Join With Segments button in the Node Edit Roll-Up. Repeat this process with the two left corresponding nodes.

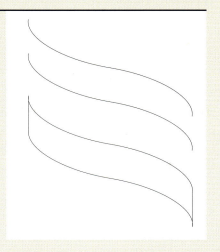

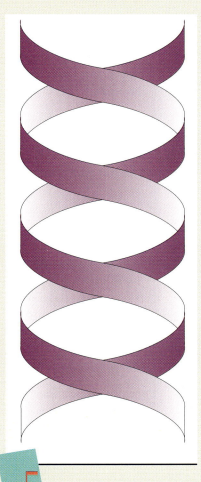

4 Open the Transform Roll-Up. Click on the Scale and Mirror button. Click on the Horizontal Mirror button. Click on the Apply To Duplicate button. Fill with a gradient fill of your choice, as shown here.

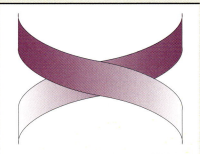

5 Set Place duplicates and clones to Horizontal 0 inches and Vertical –1.4 inches. Duplicate the two ribbon objects several times. Fill with a gradient fill of your choice.

Positioning Objects with Spirals

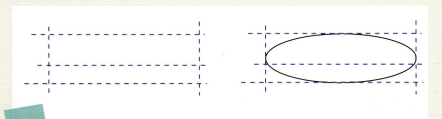

1 Place two vertical guidelines 3 inches apart, and two horizontal guidelines 1 inch apart. Place another horizontal guideline .375 inches above the lower guideline. With Snap To Guidelines on, within the guidelines, draw a 1-inch-high by 3-inch-wide oval. Convert To Curves.

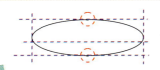

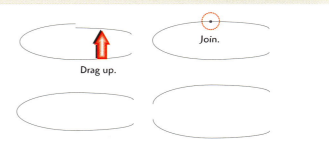

2
Open the Node Edit Roll-Up. With the Shape Tool, select the top-middle and bottom-middle nodes. Click on the Break Node button in the Node Edit Roll-Up. Press Ctrl+K to break apart both nodes. You now have two ellipse segments—one on the left and another on the right.

3
Select the ellipse segment on the right. Drag the top-middle bounding box down to the .375-inch guideline. Shift+select the two ellipse segments. Combine them. With the Shape Tool, marquee-select the two nodes where the combined segments meet. Click on the Join Nodes button in the Node Edit Roll-Up.

4
Break Apart the nodes on the right and left, as indicated.

5
Drag the top-right segment up so that it connects to the top-left segment. Combine the segments. Join the nodes where they intersect.

At this point, you should have two segments. The segments on the right are for illustration purposes only. Do not separate segments as shown here.

6
In Options, set Place duplicates and clones to Horizontal 0 inches and Vertical -.25 inches. Duplicate each segment once.

7
Make each pair a closed path. Draw lines between the ends. Combine the lines and segments. Join the intersecting nodes. Or use the Join With Segments feature in the Node Edit Roll-Up as in the previous examples. When you are finished, you should have two objects.

8
Fill each object with a gradient fill, as shown here. Keeping a thin outline on the spiral will help define the spiral's shape.

9 In Options, set Place duplicates and clones to Horizontal 0 inches and Vertical -.625 inches. Select both objects. Duplicate several times.

10 You can easily make an object or line appear to be in the middle of the spiral by positioning the object on top of the spiral. Shift+select all of the front spiral objects. Send them To Front (Shift+PgUp).

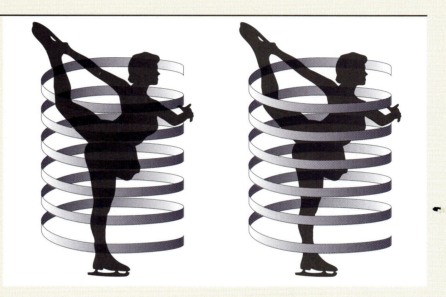

VARIATION
This can also be accomplished with the spiral ribbon.

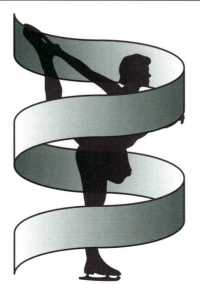

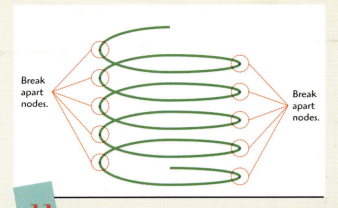

Break apart nodes.

Break apart nodes.

11 To accomplish this effect with the spiral line, you must break apart all of the left and right nodes.

12 Once the spiral is split up into segments, you can accomplish the effect in the same way as shown in the examples here.

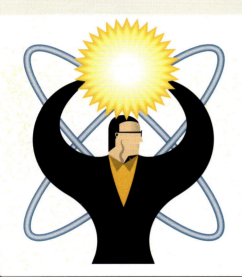

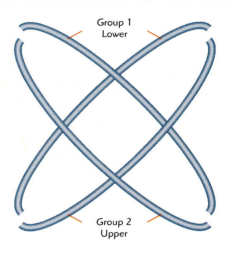

Group 1
Lower

Group 2
Upper

VARIATION

A slight variation of this effect was used on the cover illustration. The man and the ball of light were positioned over the neon ellipse bands.

The lower and upper sets of bands were grouped. Then, the upper set of bands was sent to the front. (See Project 8 for a discussion of the neon effect.)

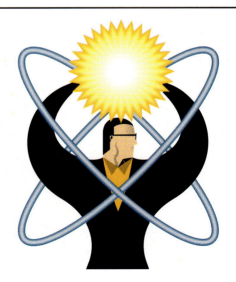

Creating Curved Arrows

Add nodes.

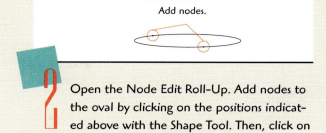

1 Draw an ellipse 2 inches wide and .25 inches high. Convert To Curves.

2 Open the Node Edit Roll-Up. Add nodes to the oval by clicking on the positions indicated above with the Shape Tool. Then, click on the Plus (+) button in the Node Edit Roll-Up.

Break apart nodes.

3 Break apart the nodes that you just added and the node on the left, as indicated here. Delete the ellipse segment on the right. After completing this step, you should have two segments. The two segments you should have separated are shown here for illustration purposes only. Do not separate segments.

4 Set Place duplicates and clones to Horizontal 0 inches and Vertical -.20 inches. Duplicate both segments once.

5 Draw lines between corresponding nodes in each segment. Combine the lines and segments. Join the nodes. Or use the Join With Segments feature in the Node Edit Roll-Up. When you finish this step, you should have two objects.

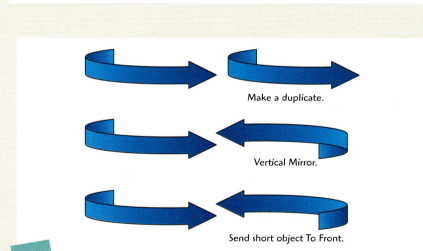

Make a duplicate.

Vertical Mirror.

Send short object To Front.

6 Place a triangle at the end of the longer object as indicated. Shift+select the triangle and the longer object. Select Arrange ➢ Weld. Fill the objects with gradient fills.

7 The curved arrow can also appear to be turning in the opposite direction. Make a duplicate of the two curved arrow objects by selecting both of them. Ctrl+drag to the right about 2 inches, then click on the right mouse button. Vertically and horizontally mirror the duplicate curved arrow objects using the Transform Roll-Up. Send the shorter object To Front. Group each pair of curved arrow objects.

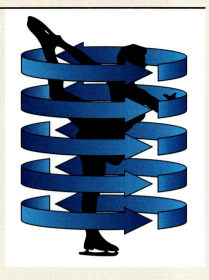

8 If you reposition the second pair of curved objects as shown here, the arrows will go in a full circle.

9 You can accomplish the same effect with the curved arrows as was shown earlier with the spirals.

Creating Flags

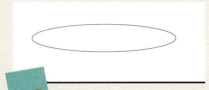

1 Draw an ellipse approximately 1.5 inches wide and .33 inches high. Convert To Curves.

2 Break apart the ellipse, as indicated here.

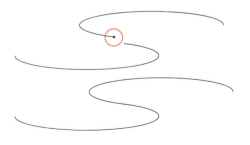

3 Create a duplicate of the ellipse segment by pressing Ctrl+D. Mirror the duplicate horizontally and vertically using the Scale and Mirror option in the Transform Roll-Up. Turn on Snap To Objects. Select all of the nodes in the duplicate segment with the Shape Tool. Click on the node indicated above (circled). Drag the duplicate segment into position, as shown here. Combine the two segments. Join the intersecting nodes.

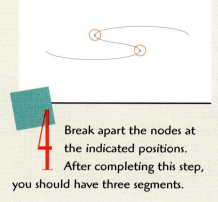

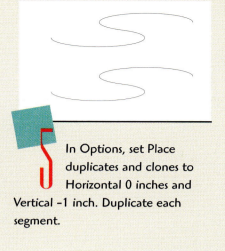

4 Break apart the nodes at the indicated positions. After completing this step, you should have three segments.

5 In Options, set Place duplicates and clones to Horizontal 0 inches and Vertical –1 inch. Duplicate each segment.

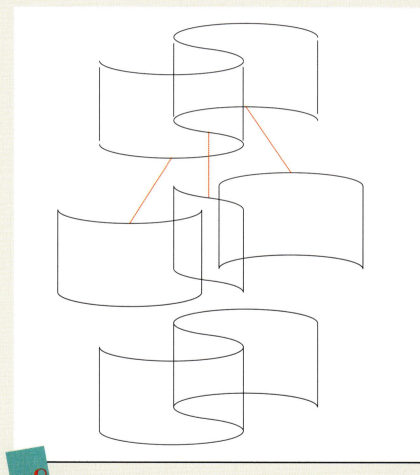

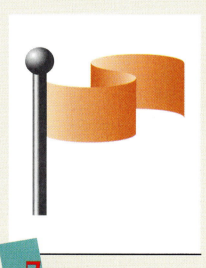

6 Draw lines between corresponding nodes in each segment. Combine the lines and segments. Join the nodes.

Or use Join With Segments feature in the Node Edit Roll-Up. When you finish this step, you should have three objects.

7 Fill the objects with gradients as shown here. Add a flag pole, and you've got a flag.

Creating Lines from Squares

Lest you think that squares are useless for creating lines, let's look at one last tidbit.

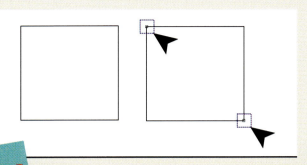

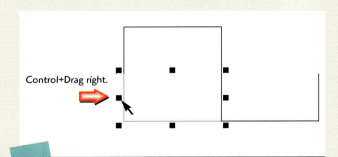

Control+Drag right.

1 Draw a 1-inch square. Convert it to curves. Click on the Shape Tool. Marquee-select the top-left node. Open the Node Edit Roll-Up. Click once on the Plus (+) button. This should add a node exactly in the middle of the left side of the square between the top-left and bottom-left nodes. Repeat this process with the bottom-right node to add a node in the middle of the right side of the square. Select both of the nodes you just created. Break apart the nodes.

2 With the Pick Tool, click on the lower half of the square segment. Click on the middle-left bounding box. Ctrl+drag to the right to create a horizontal mirror of the lower segment.

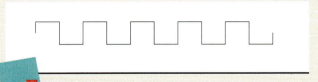

3 Combine the two half-square segments. Join the overlapping nodes. In Options, set Place duplicates and clones to Horizontal –2 inches and Vertical 0 inches. Duplicate several times. Not too exciting, but it's the beginnings of a castle wall.

The point of all this is that useful lines can be created from basic shapes with little effort. Many of these techniques are the foundation for more complex techniques, as we shall see in some of the following projects.

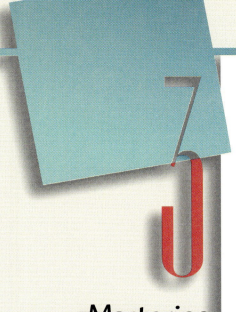

Mastering Decorative Line Techniques

What you will learn

- Working with PowerLines

- Using Blend

- Enhancing with the "woodcut" look

- Creating random and irregular lines and shapes

orelDRAW's ability to create attractive, decorative lines is greatly enhanced by using such features as PowerLines and Blend. These features can create a multitude of line effects. The basic technique is easy, and the following examples are only a small representation of the types of lines you can create.

Working with PowerLines

Draw a .25-inch line. Duplicate it by pressing the Plus (+) key. Ctrl+drag the duplicate 2 inches to the right. Select both segments. Blend with five steps. (Note that the new segment should stay on the same vertical plane through the duplicate, drag, and blend steps.) With the group still selected, choose Separate from the Arrange menu. Click off the lines. Click back on the blended portion. Choose Ungroup from the Arrange menu. Then select all of the line segments. Combine them by pressing Ctrl+L.

Place a horizontal guideline about an inch below the segments. With Snap To Guidelines on, Ctrl+drag the combined segments to the guidelines. Then click on the right mouse button to place a duplicate on the guideline.

Open the PowerLine Roll-Up (Ctrl+F8). Click on the far left button. Select a shape and a Max Width setting. (In this example, the shape selected is Wedge1 at .25 Max Width.) Click Apply. Although PowerLines are considered "lines," they also have fills. Select a fill and outline for the PowerLine.

Repeat step 2 to place another copy of the combined segments on top of the one to which you just applied the PowerLines. If the new combined segments are not on top of the PowerLine segments, press Shift+PgUp to send To Front. Apply a different PowerLine to these segments. The example here was created by applying the same shape with progressively smaller Max Width settings.

VARIATIONS

If you want the "segments" to touch, use the above method to add the PowerLines, but try the following method to create the line segments. Draw a straight line several inches long. Open the Node Edit Roll-Up. Select both nodes with the Shape Tool. Click two or three times on the Add Node button. With all of the nodes still selected, click on the Break Node button in the Node Edit Roll-Up.

Once you have created the line segments and selected them with the Pick Tool, you can follow steps 3 and 4 above to add PowerLines and additional layers.

When using segments that connect, there is no reason you can't use lines that have different numbers of segments on them.

The Bullet3 PowerLine setting can be used to make dotted lines. Simply make sure the Max Width setting is the same as the length of the line segment.

Finally, you certainly aren't limited to using solid fills or straight lines. Try this technique with Texture Fills, curved lines, and even text. In addition, CorelDRAW allows you to create your own custom PowerLine shapes.

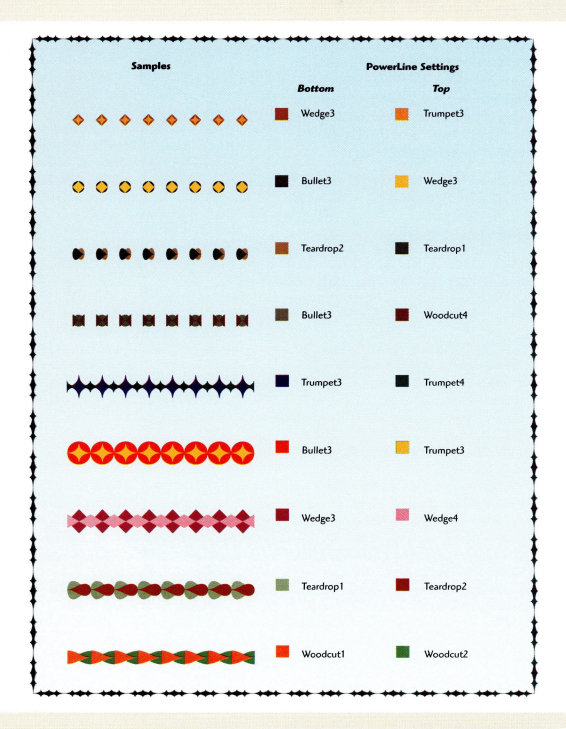

Samples	PowerLine Settings			
	Bottom		**Top**	
	■	Wedge3	■	Trumpet3
	■	Bullet3	■	Wedge3
	■	Teardrop2	■	Teardrop1
	■	Bullet3	■	Woodcut4
	■	Trumpet3	■	Trumpet4
	■	Bullet3	■	Trumpet3
	■	Wedge3	■	Wedge4
	■	Teardrop1	■	Teardrop2
	■	Woodcut1	■	Woodcut2

Using Blend

The Blend function can be applied to objects and lines to create unique, attractive lines. Groups of objects can also be blended, so you can use as many objects and lines as you need or desire.

Begin with any combination of shapes and lines you like. Group the objects and lines if you have more than one of each by marquee-selecting all of them. Choose Arrange ➢ Group. Select the object, line, or group of objects and/or lines. Ctrl+drag it to the right a few inches. Before releasing the left mouse button, click on the right mouse button to make a duplicate.

Select both the original and the copy. Select Effects ➢ Blend Roll-Up, or press Ctrl+B. Blend between the two copies with about ten steps.

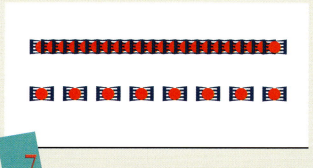

You can vary the decorative line result by increasing or decreasing the number of Blend steps.

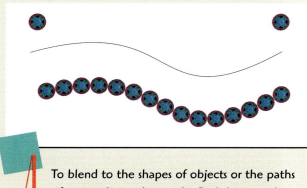

To blend to the shapes of objects or the paths of various lines, choose the Path button, then the New Path feature on the Blend Roll-Up.

Enhancing with the "Woodcut" Look

The very popular "woodcut" look can be achieved by blending shapes to create highlights and/or shadows.

1 Double-click on the Polygon Tool. In the Tool Properties dialog box, under the General tab, click on the Polygon option. Enter 3 in the Number of Points option. Click OK. Click and drag the mouse to draw a triangle about .2 inches wide and .75 inches high. Convert it to curves by pressing Ctrl+Q.

WARNING

Only CorelDRAW 6 has the Polygon Tool. To create a triangle in earlier versions, draw a rectangle about .2 inches wide and .75 inches high. Convert To Curves. Select the upper-right node. Click on the Add Node button in the Node Edit Roll-Up. Delete the upper-left and upper-right nodes.

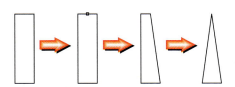

2 Duplicate the triangle. Ctrl+drag it to the right several inches. Blend between the triangles. If the first Blend steps you use do not overlap each triangle, keep adding triangles (i.e., more Blend steps) until they do overlap.

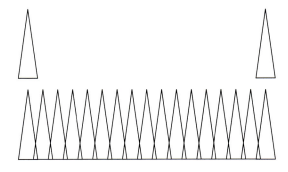

3 Separate and Ungroup the blended spikes. Select all of them. Then select Weld from the Arrange menu.

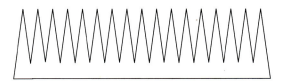

4 This technique was used to add the shading to this woodcut-stylized pen.

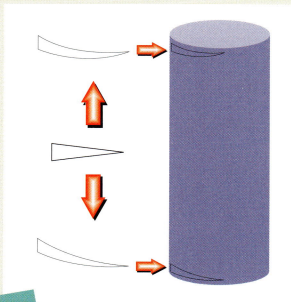

5 To create circular objects, simply convert the tri-angle to curves and conform two copies of the triangle to the shape of the top and bottom of the circular object. The triangular shapes will usually be slightly different from each other.

6 Select both curved spike shapes. Blend. Separate and Ungroup the blend. Weld the shapes together.

7 You can fill the woodcut shape with a lighter color for highlights or a darker color for shadow effects.

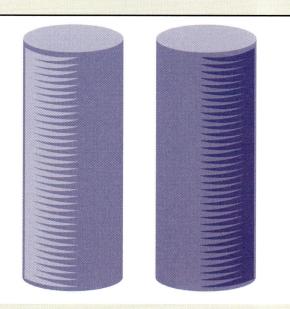

8 The woodcut effect can be used to add depth to an illustration. Woodcut shading on this simple safe illustration makes it appear as though it is bulging slightly. The woodcut effect can also add style to otherwise lackluster illustrations.

Creating Random and Irregular Lines and Shapes

Here's one final technique for creating lines. Lines in vector-based programs like CorelDRAW are so precise that they give away the fact they were created on the computer. With the following techniques, you can create lines that are more random or irregular.

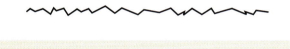

1 Draw a straight line. Select the Shape Tool. Marquee-select both nodes. Click four times on the Plus (+) button in the Node Edit Roll-Up to add 15 evenly spaced nodes to the line.

2 Now select each node individually, and manually and randomly reposition each one.

3 Using this technique, random borders can be given to squares and other shapes.

4

Creating
Shapes
with Lines

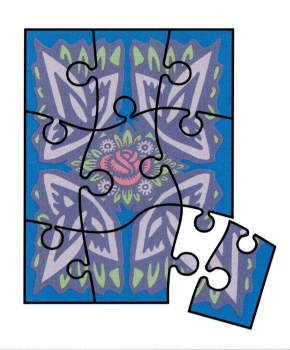

What you will learn

- Making shapes with lines

- Sculpting with lines

- Working with lines to trim shapes with holes

- Trimming text, fonts, and symbols

- Mastering even more spirals

- Creating design elements and backgrounds

- Creating pie charts with lines

L ines can be used to create shapes with the assistance of the Trim feature found on the Arrange menu. In many instances, this technique can be used to render in minutes shapes that would take hours using other methods.

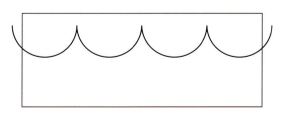

Draw a rectangle 2.5 inches wide and 1 inch high. Recreate the wave line as shown in Project 2. Center the line over the rectangle as shown.

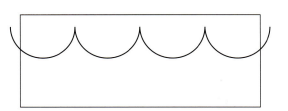

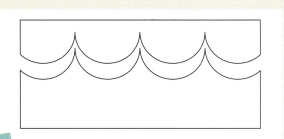

2 Select the line with the Pick Tool. Shift+select the rectangle. Select Trim from the Arrange menu. The Trim Roll-Up appears. With nothing checked under Leave Original, click on the Trim button. A large black arrow appears. Point it at the rectangle, and click. At this point, it may not look like much has happened.

3 Select Break Apart from the Arrange menu (Ctrl+K). Click off the object. Click back on the lower segment. Drag it away slightly.

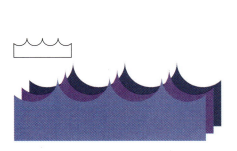

4 Now you've got waves...Or perhaps part of a curtain.

Sculpting with Lines

Using lines, you can sculpt out any variety of shapes from squares, rectangles, circles, and ellipses.

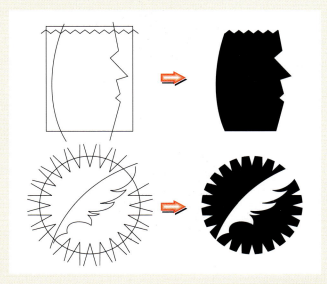

Working with Lines to Trim Shapes with Holes

There are some limitations and caveats you should be aware of when trimming with lines.

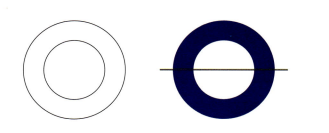

1 To experience one limitation, draw a perfect circle by choosing the Ellipse Tool and pressing Ctrl as you drag the mouse. Create an inner duplicate by opening the Transform Roll-Up (Alt+F9). In the Scale section, enter Horizontal 70% and Vertical 70%. Click on Apply To Duplicate. Select both circles. Combine them (Ctrl+L). Fill them with any color by clicking on a color displayed at the bottom of the screen with the left mouse button. Draw a straight line and center it over the O shape.

2 Select the line. Shift+select the donut shape. Select Trim from Arrange menu. At first, it looks like you've trimmed the donut in half ...

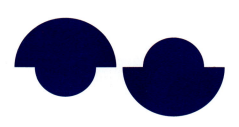

3 ...But, when you break apart the trimmed donut shape, you will find that you've created two odd-looking shapes instead of two half-donut shapes. We will look at how to cut a donut in half in Project 6.

There is another limitation to be aware of. Occasionally, trimming a closed path does not always result in two closed paths as in the previous example. If a path is not closed after trimming, locate the point at which the nodes are not joined and join them.

Trimming Text

Although CorelDRAW cannot trim shapes that have holes in them with a line, it can trim text with a line. This is true even if the text is converted to curves—which, in effect, makes it just like any other shape created with shape tools.

OOPS!

1 Click on the Artistic Text Tool. Click on the layout, and type the word *OOPS!* in all caps. (You can type any word you wish; *OOPS!* just happens to have plenty of counters, or holes, in the letters O and P.) Draw a straight horizontal line through the word as shown here.

2 Select the line. Shift+select the word. Select Trim from the Arrange menu. Proceed as before. Use the line to Trim the word. Select Break Apart from the Arrange menu. Marquee-select all of the top half-letters. Choose Combine from the Arrange menu. Combine all of the bottom half as well. Fill each half with a different color to show that they are now separate objects.

3 Delete the line. You now have two halves of the word to play with. In this case, the center of rotation was moved on the top object, and the object was rotated slightly. This is done by double-clicking on the top object, moving the center of rotation, clicking on the handle, and rotating the object slightly.

Trimming Fonts and Symbols

The ability to trim text with lines extends to clipart fonts and CorelDRAW's symbols. This serves as an efficient workaround for CorelDRAW's limitation with shapes that have holes in them. If the shape is not too complex, you can make it into a symbol. Then you will be able to trim the shape with a line.

1 To see this, recreate the donut-shaped object. With the donut-shaped object selected, select Tools ➢ Create ➢ Symbol. Enter a new name in the Symbol Category, such as Art 1, so that you can easily find the shape in the Symbols Roll-Up.

HINT

The Symbols Roll-Up always opens up to the Symbol Category that is first in alphabetical order. If that Symbol Category has complex shapes in it, the Symbols Roll-Up will open more slowly when you need it. A simple solution to this annoyance is to create a symbol with a basic shape, such as a circle or square, and make a separate Symbol Category for it with a title such as "AAA."

So long as this Symbol Category is first in alphabetical order, it will be displayed when the Symbols Roll-Up is opened, and, because of the simple shape, the Symbols Roll-Up will open faster.

2 Now drag and drop the donut shape from the Symbols Roll-Up (Ctrl+F11). Draw a straight horizontal line over the donut shape. Trim the donut shape with the line.

Delete the line. Select Break Apart from the Arrange menu. In the example here, the shapes have been filled with different colors to show that they are now different shapes.

Mastering Even More Spirals

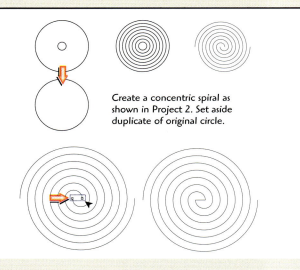

Create a concentric spiral as shown in Project 2. Set aside duplicate of original circle.

1 Here you will be creating a concentric spiral; but first, make a duplicate of the larger original circle that you will use to make the concentric spirals. Then, create a concentric spiral as demonstrated in Project 2. But, do not break apart and delete the extra spiral. After

you've rendered the concentric spirals, you will have two combined sets of spirals with all overlapping nodes joined. Now, draw a line between the two inside ends. Combine the new line with the spiral. Join the nodes. The result should be one line with no nodes broken apart.

2 Position the concentric spiral over the duplicate circle. Select the concentric spiral. Shift+select the circle. Select Trim from the Arrange menu.

Duplicate from outer original circle used to create the concentric spiral.

3 Delete the concentric spiral. Select the trimmed circle. Break it apart. Delete the line. Fill the spirals with two different colors to make them easier to select.

A complex line like the concentric spiral is a prime example of the kind of line for which CorelDRAW may not be able to close the path. If your spirals do not fill with the selected color, it means that the path is not closed and you will need to manually join the nodes where the path remains open.

4 If you delete one of the spirals, you have a nice spiral that tapers off at one end. You can also delete a few nodes at the inside end and round off the end by editing the Beziér curves.

Creating Design Elements and Backgrounds

1 This technique is particularly useful for creating design elements and backgrounds. Draw a 1.5-inch square. Next, draw a 2.25-inch straight line. Center it over the square.

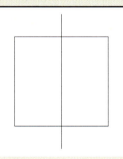

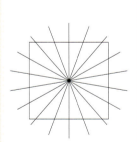

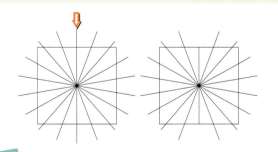

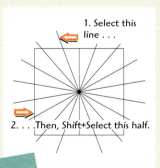

1. Select this line . . .

2. . . . Then, Shift+Select this half.

2 Open the Transform Roll-Up, and select the Rotate card (Alt+F8). In Angle:, enter 20 degrees. Click eight times on the Apply To Duplicate button.

3 To trim all of the lines out of the square is a bit tricky and tedious. First, select the center vertical line. Shift+select the square. Select Trim. When you delete the line and break apart the trimmed square, you will have two halves. From this point on, you will have to trim both halves with every other line.

4 Select the next line to the left. Shift+select the left half of the trimmed square. Select Trim. Do not delete the line yet because you will need it for the other half. Break apart the newly trimmed left rectangle.

5 Select the same line again. Shift+select the right half of the original trimmed square. Select Trim. Now you can delete the line because you have trimmed both halves with it. Break apart the newly trimmed right rectangle.

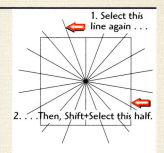

1. Select this line again . . .

2. . . .Then, Shift+Select this half.

6 Repeat the two previous steps with the remaining lines.

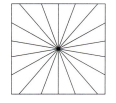

7 For a quick way to check if there are any unclosed paths, select all of the trimmed objects and fill them with a color. Those sections that do not fill need to be closed.

8 Once all the paths are closed, you have the framework for an attractive design element or background.

Creating Pie Charts

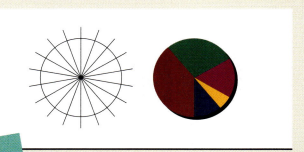

1 The rotated straight-lines technique can also be used to create pie charts. You do not need to trim every line from every section.

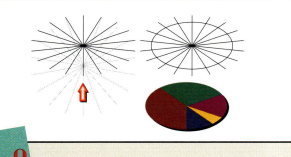

2 To apply this technique to an ellipse for oval pie charts, vertically scale the rotated lines to better orient them for the ellipse.

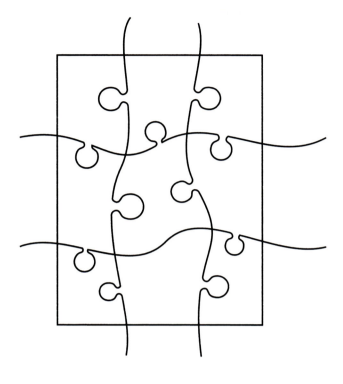

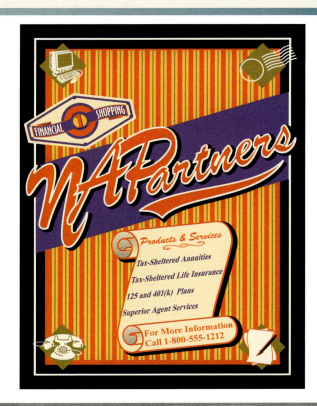

Extruding and Contouring Shapes from Lines

What you will learn

- Extruding a booklet or a book

- Making scrolls, rolled-up dollar bills, and banners

- Creating realistic corrugated metal

- Contouring shapes from lines

t is so easy to extrude text that CorelDRAW's Extrude effect often does not get used for much of anything else. However, you can enhance your work by mastering some of these techniques.

Extruding a Booklet or a Book

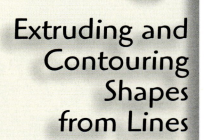

To extrude a shape from a line, start with a basic line like the one above. Press Ctrl+E to open the Extrude Roll-Up. Click on the second button from the left (the extruded box icon). Now everything you need for this technique is right in front of you.

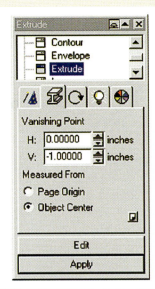

2 Select Back Parallel from the first drop-down menu. Select VP (vanishing point) Locked To Object from the second menu. Click on the tiny page icon in the lower right-hand portion of the Extrude Roll-Up to adjust the Vanishing Point Coordinates.

3 The extrude should go directly downward, so click on Object Center under Measured From. Enter 0 for the horizontal setting. Next, enter a value for the vertical setting: negative numbers extrude down, and positive numbers extrude up. Press Apply to extrude the line.

4 Choose Separate from the Arrange menu. Click off the selected item. Click back on. Choose Ungroup from the Arrange menu. Delete the original line, and you have a useful shape that would have been relatively difficult to create with the Pencil and/or Shape Tools.

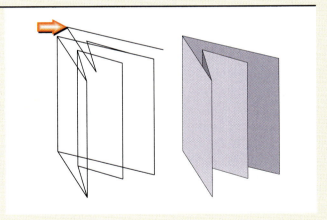

VARIATION

A slight variation creates a book.

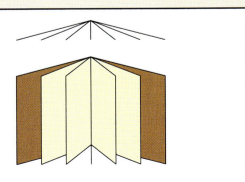

Making Scrolls,
Rolled-up Dollar Bills, and Banners

1 A scroll shape can be created easily using the same technique. In this case, the vertical vanishing point was set to 0, and the horizontal vanishing point was set to about 1.25 inches.

2 The results of the Extrude process often take some cleaning up in order to use the shape. When CorelDRAW extrudes curves, it uses an excessive number of nodes to render the curve. Delete these extra nodes if they make your drawing so complex that it won't print.

Also, in the particular case of the scroll, each half-circle curve is made up of two pieces. To make the scroll more realistic, delete the extra nodes, then use Weld to combine the two half-circles.

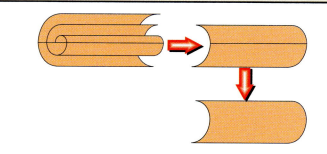

3 CorelDRAW makes a shape for each pair of nodes. If you don't want two halves, you can safely delete the middle node, since a half-circle only needs two nodes to render accurately. Now, when you extrude, only one shape will be created.

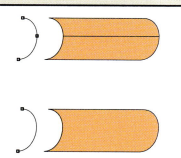

4 All that work on the half-circles pays off with the insides of the scroll, where you can add gradients for shading.

You can use this technique to create a rolled-up dollar bill, a banner, and much more.

The illustration below utilized the extruding lines technique heavily. The ribbon, scroll, and wavy paper were all rendered with extruded lines.

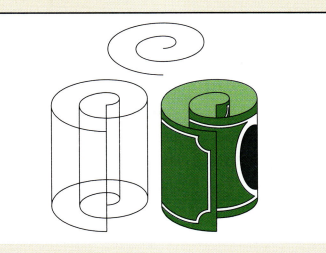

Creating Realistic Corrugated Metal

Although lines have no closed paths, they can be filled with any fill you wish, which will come in handy with this next technique. Simply construct a wavy line, fill it with a custom linear gradient fill as shown here, and extrude. (See Project 9 for a discussion of custom linear fills.) Remove the original line and outline, and you have a realistic-looking piece of corrugated metal. Use brown tones for corrugated cardboard.

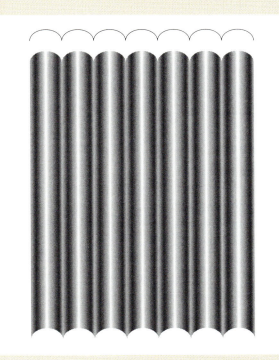

Of course, the extrude tool is also useful for extruding text. In this case, the extrusions of the words "FLEXPLUS™ Benefit Management Systems" were filled with custom fills to help give the extrusions more depth and more accurate shading.

Contouring Shapes from Lines

It's mostly an oddity, but the Contour Tool can contour lines to make shapes. Doing a simple exercise will familiar-ize you with this technique.

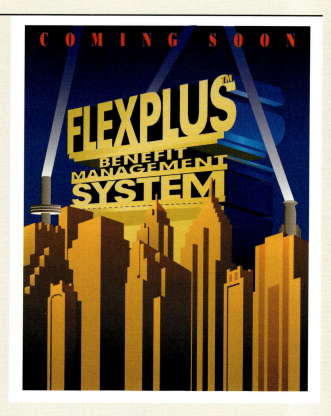

1. Draw a short, straight line. With the line still selected, open the Contour Roll-Up from the Effects menu (Ctrl+F9). Outside is the only option available for contouring lines. Set the Offset to .1, and Steps to 1. Click on Apply. Note that contoured lines have strange notches at the end. Also, to isolate the new shape, you will need to Separate and Ungroup it from the line.

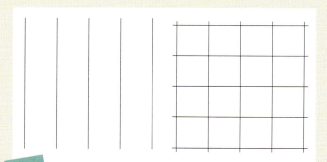

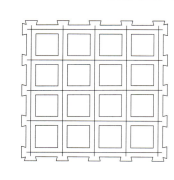

2. Becoming familiar with a few practical applica-tions of this technique will expand your creative possibilities. Draw a vertical straight line just over 2 inches long. In Options, set Place duplicates and clones to Horizontal 2 inches and Vertical 0 inches. Duplicate the line. Select both lines. Blend between them with three steps. Separate and Ungroup the steps. Combine the lines. Open the Transform Roll-Up. Enter 90 degrees in the Rotate card. Select Apply To Duplicate. Combine the new set of rotated lines with the original set.

3. Apply a single-step contour to the line with an offset of .75 inches. It may not look like much, but...

4 ...With a little dressing up, it can be a useful map. The center line was adjusted to create a curve. Any adjustments to the original line will result in the contour being updated automatically. After the line was adjusted, the contour was separated from the line and filled with gray. Once you Separate and Ungroup the contour, however, it will no longer update. The line was then changed to a dashed white line, and then both lines and contours were PowerClipped into a green square.

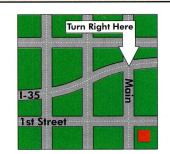

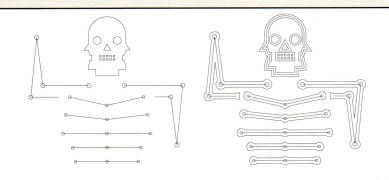

V A R I A T I O N

Contouring lines can be used for creating much more than maps. These skeletal lines and shapes were combined, then contoured to create bones.

Duplicates of this simple line were created when it was rotated around an axis. Then a five-step contour was added to create an interesting background pattern.

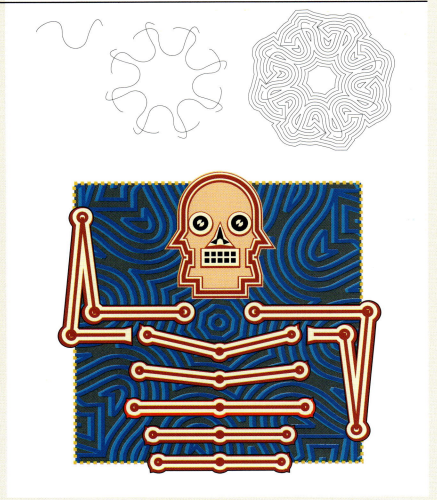

Using Weld, Trim, and Combine to Create Shapes

What you will learn

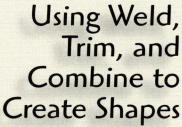

- Creating shapes with weld

- Putting together illustrations

- Trimming shapes

- Trimming shapes with holes

- Using shapes to trim lines

- Digital sculpting with Weld and Trim

- Using concentric step-and-repeat techniques

Starting with simplified shapes and editing them into more complex masterpieces is an effective way to master CorelDRAW. With the above simple shapes (or variations of them), you can create just about any other shape you like by using Weld, Trim, Intersection, and Combine. With these tools, you can create the foundation for your work, and then edit the shapes. You can also add colors, highlights, shadows, or whatever else your illustration needs.

Creating shapes with the Weld feature is pure simplicity. Position objects so they overlap. Select them all. Then, choose Weld from the Arrange menu. If the result is

not quite what you want or if the shape does not weld because objects were not overlapping, select Undo, move the shapes around a little, and try again. Usually, the most difficult thing about welding is creating and arranging the shapes to be welded.

IMPORTANT NOTE: The Weld feature was introduced in CorelDRAW 4. Trim and Intersection were both introduced in CorelDRAW 5. CorelDRAW 6 treats Weld, Trim, and Intersection slightly different from versions 4 (for Weld) and 5. See the Introduction for a discussion of Weld, Trim, and Intersection and their differences in each CorelDRAW version.

Creating Shapes with Weld

Here are the steps for welding a lightning bolt, followed by several variations to show you Weld's potential.

1 Draw a rectangle .35 inches wide and .75 inches high. Press Alt+F11 to open the Skew controls. Enter Horizontal 0 degrees and Vertical 30 degrees. Press the Apply button. Convert the skewed rectangle to curves.

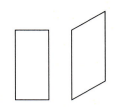

2 Make a duplicate of the skewed rectangle. Set aside the original. Open the Node Edit Roll-Up. Select the skewed rectangle with the Shape Tool. Select the upper-right node. Press the Add Node button in the Node Edit Roll-Up. Select the upper-right node with the Shape Tool. Delete the node. Select the upper-left node with the Shape Tool. Delete the node. This is a skewed triangle.

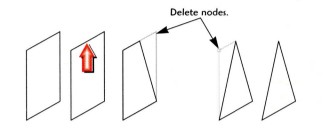

Delete nodes.

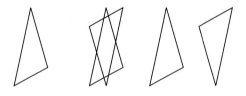

3 Open the Scale and Mirror controls (Alt+F9). Select the Horizontal and Vertical Mirror buttons. Press the Apply To Duplicate button.

4 Arrange the skewed rectangle and the two skewed triangles as shown here. To weld them together to form a lightning bolt, first select all the elements. Then choose Arrange ➢ Weld. Click on Weld To on the Weld Roll-Up. Point the black arrow at the rectangle.

This cactus was created by drawing five circles and five rectangles, then positioning them so that they overlapped at each junction. Getting the rotation of the two angled rectangles just right was the only difficulty in creating this image. On the first try, the upper-right circle did not weld like the rest of the shapes. Undo was selected, the circle was repositioned slightly, and then the shapes were rewelded.

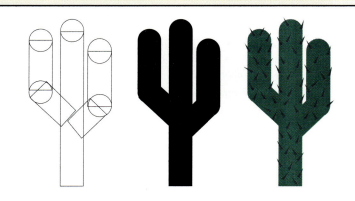

Sometimes Weld may not be able to weld a particular odd shape. The Weld feature can also get overwhelmed with too many shapes. You may need to weld only a few shapes at a time, or even weld some shapes before others. For example, the ellipses on these musical notes had to be welded to the long rectangles before all of them could be welded to the larger curved rectangle. The point is that you may need to try different welding strategies to get objects to weld together correctly.

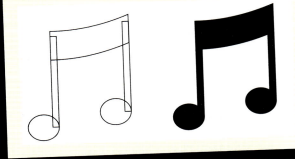

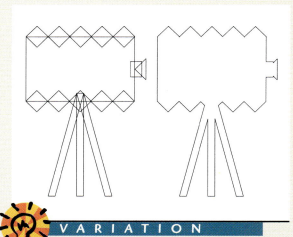

This seemingly more complex shape welded perfectly on the first try.

When welding shapes, any shape that is completely surrounded by another will disappear after welding. For example, the eyes and mouth of the alien disappeared after all the shapes were welded together.

The exception to this rule is when a shape has a hole in it. The two eye shapes here have been combined to form a single shape. Once the combining is done, the circle can be welded to the new eye shape without disappearing. The monster mouth was created in the same way.

The eyeball shape can be created using the techniques presented in Project 2. The eyeball shape was created by converting a circle to curves, breaking apart the nodes, and then using one of the resulting segments. The segment was rotated, then a Mirror copy of it was made. The two segments were Combined, the nodes were joined, and a contour was added. The contour was Separated, Ungrouped, then Combined with the original eyeball shape.

Use the Combine feature to make the eyes, mouth, and face into one object.

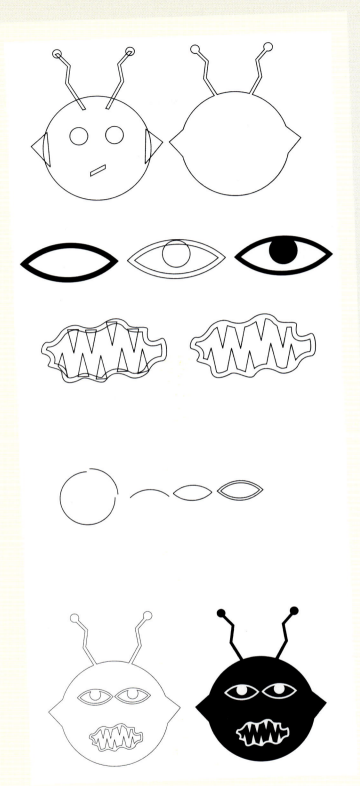

Weld can be the key to entire illustrations. This illustration was created completely from welded shapes.

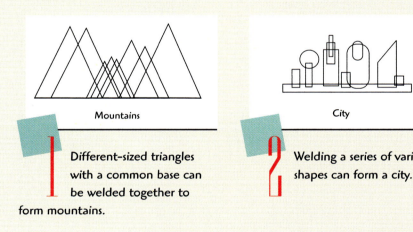

Mountains

1 Different-sized triangles with a common base can be welded together to form mountains.

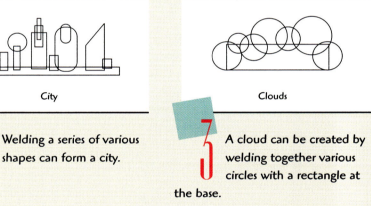

City

2 Welding a series of various shapes can form a city.

Clouds

3 A cloud can be created by welding together various circles with a rectangle at the base.

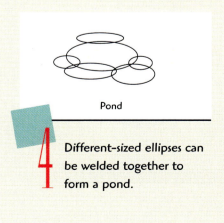

Pond

4 Different-sized ellipses can be welded together to form a pond.

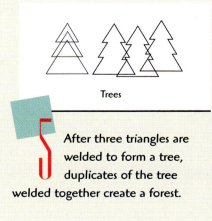

Trees

5 After three triangles are welded to form a tree, duplicates of the tree welded together create a forest.

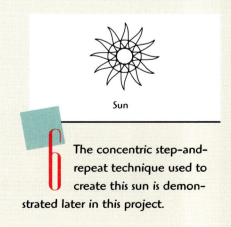

Sun

6 The concentric step-and-repeat technique used to create this sun is demonstrated later in this project.

Trimming Shapes

Trimming is almost as easy as welding. Draw a .5-inch circle. Duplicate it. Ctrl+drag it to the right about .25 inches. Select the left circle. Shift+select the right circle. Choose Trim from the Arrange menu. Proceed as described earlier by clicking on the Trim button. Position the arrow and click again.

Objects must overlap in order to trim or be trimmed. The last selected object in a Trim operation is the one that will be trimmed. If you marquee-select the object, the first object created will be trimmed.

VARIATIONS

Trims can be done with multiple objects.

Trims can be done with diagonal objects.

You can create great logos with Trim.

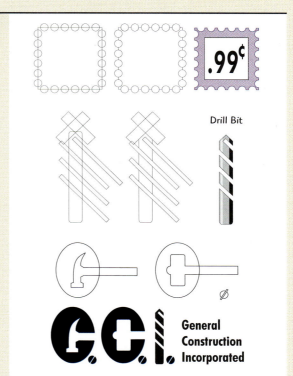

Drill Bit

C.C.I. General Construction Incorporated

Trimming Shapes with Holes

Project 4 demonstrated a limitation of the Trim feature, which is that objects with holes in them cannot be cut in half with a line. Trimming the O shape creates two odd shapes instead of creating two halves of an O. In Project 4, as an alternative, a line was used to Trim both halves of the word *OOPS!*

As discussed in Project 4, only fonts and symbols with holes in them can be trimmed with lines. Shapes with holes in them created with CorelDRAW's shape tools cannot be trimmed with lines. The following technique demonstrates another alternative to use when shapes are too cumbersome to trim with a line.

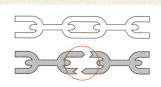

1 Draw a .5-inch circle. Select the circle with the Pick Tool. When the mouse pointer becomes a cross when positioned over the middle-left bounding box, hold down the Ctrl key, click, and drag the middle-left bounding box to the right until the circle Mirrors to the right. This will be indicated by a dotted outline appearing where you wish the new circle to be placed. While still holding down on the left mouse button, click on the right mouse button to make a duplicate. Select both circles. Combine them.

HINT

An easy way to draw shapes and lines to perfect dimensions is to use the Size feature. Draw a shape to any size, then press Alt+F10. Enter the dimensions you need. Select Apply. This works for lines as well. If the lines are perfectly horizontal or vertical, you will only be able to change one dimension.

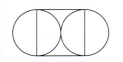 

2 Draw a perfect .5-inch square. Select the square. Shift+select the combined circles. Choose Align and Distribute (Ctrl+A) from the Arrange menu. Choose the center alignment options for both Vertical and Horizontal. Click on the Apply button. Select the combined circle and the square. Weld them together.

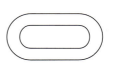

3 Select the new shape. Select the Contour Roll-Up from the Effects menu (Ctrl+F9). Change the options in the Contour Roll-Up to Inside, Offset 0.125 inches, Steps 1. Click on the Apply button. Select the contour. Choose Separate from the Arrange menu. Click off the contour. Select it again. Then, choose Ungroup from the Arrange menu. Select both shapes. Combine them. This shape will be referred to as Piece 1.

4 Set aside Piece 1. Draw a 1-inch-wide by .125-inch-high rectangle. Round the ends of the new rectangle by clicking on the upper-left node with the Shape Tool. Drag it to the right until the ends are totally rounded. This shape will be referred to as Piece 2.

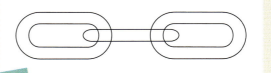

5 In Options, change Place duplicates and clones to Horizontal 1.4 inches and Vertical 0 inches. Duplicate Piece 1 one time. Group the duplicate with the original chain piece. Now, having selected both Piece 2 and the grouped chain pieces, select the Align feature from the Arrange menu. Horizontally and vertically center Piece 2 with the combined copies of Piece 1.

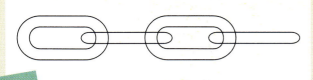

6 Select the newly centered Piece 2. Duplicate it one time.

7 To create more chain links, Ungroup the copies of Piece 1. Duplicate them. Alternate between duplicating a copy of the leftmost Piece 1 and Piece 2 as many times as it takes to create the length of chain you want. For this exercise, repeat this process until you have about seven copies of each piece. Then select all of the chain links. Resize them to about 30%.

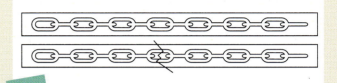

8 Now select all of the copies of Pieces 1 and 2. Weld them together. This series of chain links will be used to demonstrate the alternate trimming technique.

9 Draw a rectangle around the chain links. Now draw a jagged line across the middle of the rectangle and over an open section of the chain link. Trim the rectangle with the line. Break apart the newly trimmed rectangle.

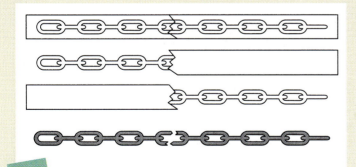

10 Press the Plus (+) key to add a duplicate of the chain links directly on top of its original. Trim one duplicate of the chain links with one half of the trimmed rectangle, and the other duplicate of the chain links with the other half of the trimmed rectangle.

1 Shapes can also be used to trim lines. Draw a 1.5-inch vertical line. Open the Rotation controls (Alt+F8). In Angle:, enter 15 degrees. Press Apply To Duplicate 12 times. Marquee-select all of the lines. Combine them.

2 Draw a .75-inch square. Center the square over the combined lines.

3 Select the square. Trim it from the combined lines. Delete the square.

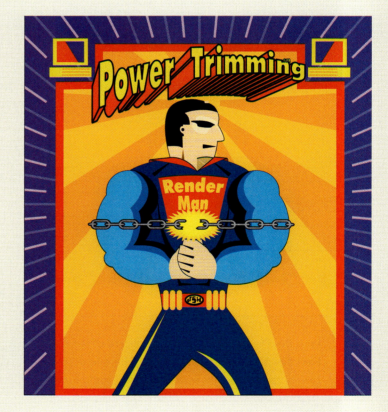

Trimming lines with shapes was used to create the streaked effect around "Render Man" in this illustration. As you can see, even simple illustrations such as the broken chain can be the key to more complex illustrations. Most complex illustrations are made up from a series of relatively simple objects and simple effects.

Digital Sculpting with Weld and Trim

Weld and Trim are very effective tools when used together. The two features can be used in conjunction with one another to digitally sculpt shapes. In the illustration here, Trim was used to create the mouth, then Weld was used to add the tongue and lower lip. After the eyes were created with Trim, the eyebrow and eye were combined.

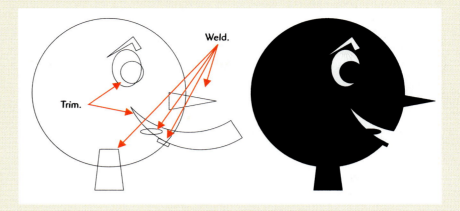

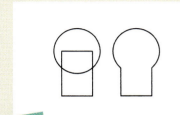

1 Draw a perfect circle about .5 inches in diameter. Draw a rectangle about .5 inches high and .33 inches wide. Position the circle and rectangle as shown here. Weld them together.

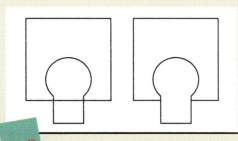

2 Draw a 1-inch square. Position one of the copies of the welded object as shown here. Trim it from the square.

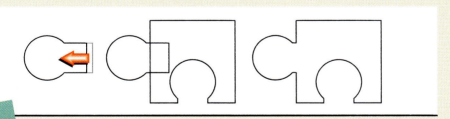

3 Rotate the welded object -90 degrees. With the Shape Tool, select the two nodes on the square end of the welded object. Nudge them to the left about .2 inches. Position the welded object as shown here. Weld it to the trimmed square.

Shapes like these can be used as the basis for icons
and other illustrations. The puzzle piece was combined with a gear shape as an icon for a company
that solved problems in the workplace.

V A R I A T I O N

Here are a few more exam-
ples of digital sculpting with Weld
and Trim.

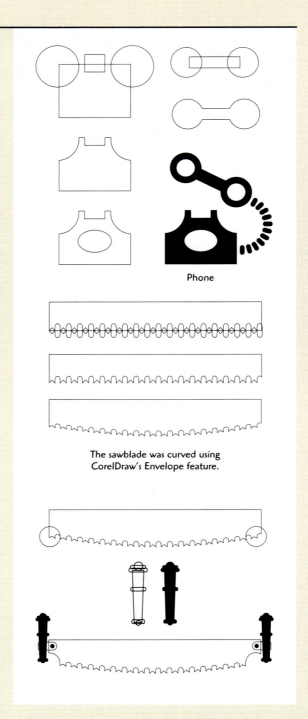

Phone

The sawblade was curved using
CorelDraw's Envelope feature.

Using Concentric Step-and-Repeat Techniques

Concentric step-and-repeat techniques are very useful when used in conjunction with Weld and Trim. Utilizing the rotation tools with the Repeat feature, you can create a variety of circular objects with Weld and Trim.

1 Place a horizontal and vertical guideline anywhere on the page. In the Layout menu, turn on the Snap To Guidelines option. You will be using the intersection of the two guidelines as the central point for the concentric step-and-repeat technique.

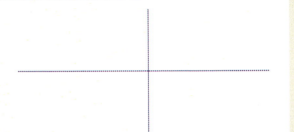

2 Select the Ellipse tool. Hold down the Shift and Ctrl keys, and click somewhere close to the intersection of the guidelines. Draw a 1.25-inch circle. With Snap To Guidelines on, the center of the circle will snap to the intersection of the guidelines.

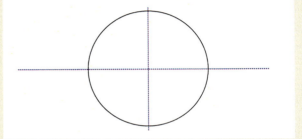

3 Off to the side, draw a small rectangle about .2 inches wide and .5 inches high. Convert the rectangle to curves. Open the Node Edit Roll-Up. Select all of the nodes with the Shape Tool. Add one node to all four sides by clicking the Add Node button in the Node Edit Roll-Up.

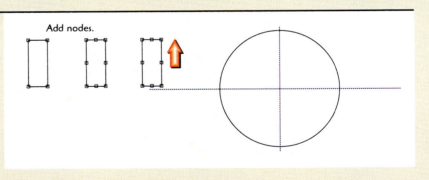

Add nodes.

4 In Options, set the Nudge value to .09 inches. Select the left-middle and right-middle nodes. Nudge them up once. In Options, set the Nudge value to .045 inches. Select the left-middle node. Nudge it left once. Select the right-middle node. Nudge it right once.

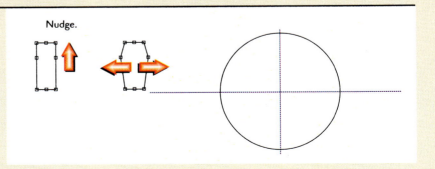

Nudge.

5 Select the manipulated rectangle. Center it over the circle. Position the manipulated rectangle so that the left-middle and right-middle nodes intersect the circle as shown here.

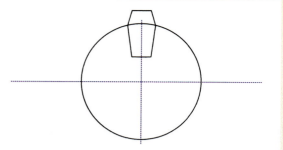

HINT

By setting the Nudge value in Options to .001 inches, you can nudge anything into place precisely. Just position your object or line as close as possible to where you want it, then nudge it into place.

6 Double-click on the manipulated rectangle to view its center of rotation. Drag the manipulated rectangle's center of rotation to the intersection of the guidelines.

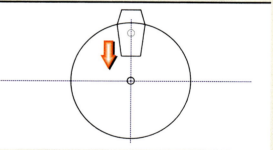

7 Open the Rotation controls (Alt+F8). In Angle:, enter 36 degrees. Press the Apply to Duplicate button. For this technique to work properly, you must enter an Angle of Rotation number that divides evenly into 360.

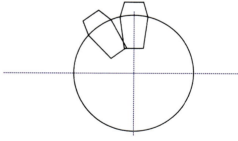

8 Press Apply to Duplicate several more times, until you have duplicates all the way around the circle.

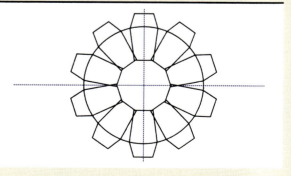

9 Select all of the copies of the manipulated rectangle and the circle. Weld them together.

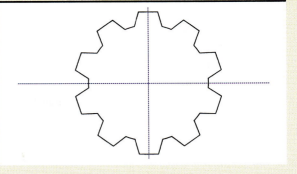

10 Select the Ellipse tool. Hold down the Shift and Ctrl keys, and click somewhere close to the intersection of the guidelines. Draw a .5-inch circle. Combine the circle and gear shape.

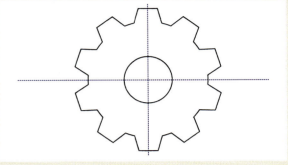

11 You can continue to make the shape even more complex. Select the Ellipse tool. Hold down the Shift and Ctrl keys, and click somewhere close to the intersection of the guidelines. Draw a 1.1-inch circle. In the same way, draw a .65-inch circle. Combine the two new circles.

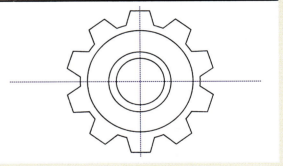

12 Draw a .075-inch-wide by 1.75-inch-high rectangle. Center it over the gear shape.

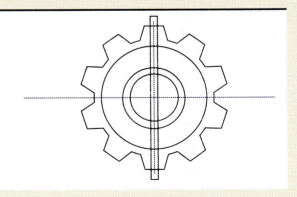

HINT

In CorelDRAW 5, double-click on the Align To Center of Page option to easily select the Horizontal and Vertical Center options in the Align dialog box.

13 Open the Rotation controls (Alt+F8). In Angle:, enter 18 degrees. Press Apply.

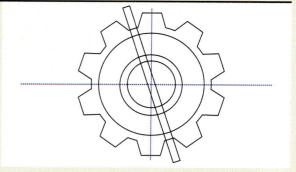

14 In Angle:, enter 36 degrees. Press Apply To Duplicate four times.

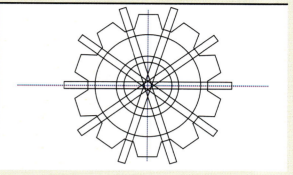

15 Select all of the rotated rectangles. Trim them from the two inner circles as shown here.

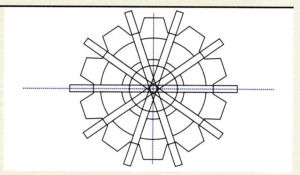

16 Delete all of the rotated rectangles. Combine the circular dashed shape with the gear shape.

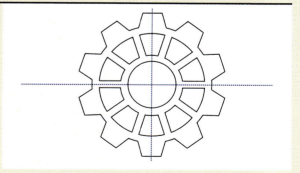

17 You could go on and on with this technique. As long as you use the guidelines as the center of rotation, you can add as many concentric elements as you want.

VARIATION

There are endless applications for this technique. Experimentation will likely yield many additional useful shapes.

Automated Rendering with Snap To Objects

What you will learn

- Beveling squares and rectangles
- Beveling polygons
- Beveling text

Beveling Squares and Rectangles

Draw a 1-inch square. Select the Contour Roll-Up from the Effects menu (Ctrl+F9). Change the Contour settings to Outside, Offset .100, and Steps 1. Press the Apply button. Separate and Ungroup the resulting contour.

HINT

To speed up color selection, create a custom color palette with these colors. Coloring objects can be easier when you have to select only from the colors you have specifically placed in the color palette.

Deep Navy Blue 40% C, 40% M, 60% K	Deep Navy Blue 30% 12% C, 12% M, 18% K
Deep Navy Blue 75% 30% C, 30% M, 45% K	Deep Navy Blue 20% 8% C, 8% M, 12% K
Deep Navy Blue 50% 20% C, 20% M, 30% K	

2 Turn on Snap To Objects in the Layout menu. Select the Beziér Tool by clicking and holding on the Freehand Tool until the flyout menu appears, and then choosing the Beziér Tool. Click on the four nodes shown above in succession. To close the path, click on the one you started with. Pay attention to the Status Bar while you are doing this. After clicking on the second node, the Status Bar will tell you that you have an Open Path. You will have an Open Path until you click on the node you started with. Once you do that, the Status Bar will no longer show Open Path, indicating that the path is now closed. A closed path is an object.

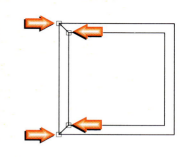

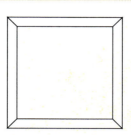

3 Repeat this process with the four other sides. When you have finished, send one of the newly created objects to the back. Delete the outer square or contour. Then, send the object you sent to the back to the front again.

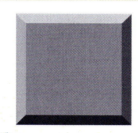

4 Fill the center square with Dark Navy Blue 50%. Fill the top bevel with Dark Navy Blue 20%. Fill the left bevel with Dark Navy Blue 30%. Fill the bottom bevel with Dark Navy Blue 100%. Fill the right bevel with Dark Navy Blue 75%.

5 Once the bevels are in place, it is very easy to resize and manipulate the beveled box. However, this works only for beveled squares and rectangles. For the purpose of this exercise, the beveled square will be shown with just the outlines.

Convert the main square to curves. With the main square still selected, select the Shape Tool. Marquee-select the two right nodes. Click on one of selected nodes with the left mouse button. Hold down the left mouse button, and drag the two nodes to the right about .5 inches.

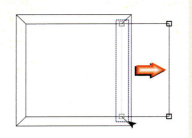

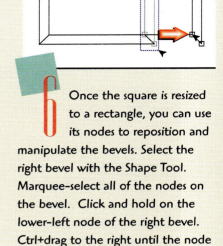

6 Once the square is resized to a rectangle, you can use its nodes to reposition and manipulate the bevels. Select the right bevel with the Shape Tool. Marquee-select all of the nodes on the bevel. Click and hold on the lower-left node of the right bevel. Ctrl+drag to the right until the node snaps to the edge of the rectangle.

7 Select the top bevel with the Shape Tool. Marquee-select the two right nodes. Click and hold on the lower-right node of the right bevel. Ctrl+drag to the right until the node snaps to the edge of the upper-right corner of the rectangle. Repeat this process for the bottom bevel using the upper-right node to drag and snap to the lower-right corner of the rectangle.

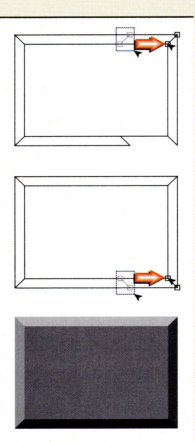

TIP

Holding down the Shift and Ctrl keys while clicking on a node selects all of the nodes on the object or line. This is handy when it is difficult to marquee-select nodes on an object or line.

Beveling Polygons

1 By themselves, lines can be used to create polygonal beveled shapes. Draw a 1.5-inch horizontal line. Open the Node Edit Roll-Up. Select both nodes on the line. Press the Add Node button twice to add three nodes to the line.

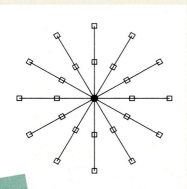

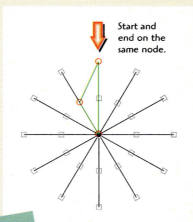

Start and end on the same node.

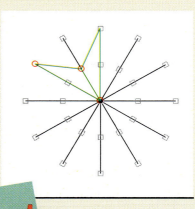

2 Open the Rotate Transform controls (Alt+F8). At Angle:, enter 30 degrees. Press the Apply To Duplicate button five times.

3 Turn on the Snap To Objects option. Click on the indicated nodes with the Beziér Tool. Start and end on the same node to create a closed path. The green line indicates the shape you should end up with.

4 Continue the process as shown above …

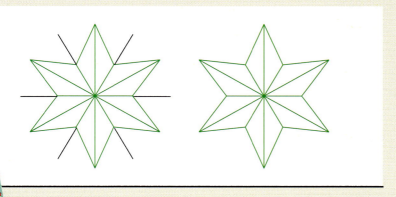

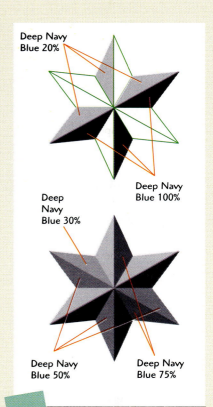

Deep Navy Blue 20%

Deep Navy Blue 100%

Deep Navy Blue 30%

Deep Navy Blue 50%

Deep Navy Blue 75%

5 … Until you have closed paths or objects that form a six-point star. When you have finished creating the closed paths, delete the lines.

6 Fill each bevel with the color indicated in the above graphic. Either delete the lines or make them the same color as the fill.

VARIATION

There are plenty of variations on this technique, depending on the angle of rotation uses and how many nodes are added to the original line.

A Five-Point Star

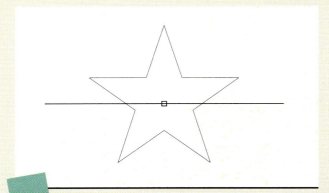

1 Use the Polygon Tool and center a line with a node added in the middle. To create a five-point star, double-click on the Polygon Tool. Under the General tab, enter 5 for Number of Points. Then, select the Polygon as Star option. Enter 50 for Sharpness. Hold down the Ctrl key when drawing the polygon/star.

2 Use the central node from the line and the corner nodes on the star to render the bevels with the Snap To Objects option on, as demonstrated earlier.

3 Fill each bevel with alternating colors. The Polygon Tool is very versatile, so any number of variations are possible with this technique.

Beveling Text

Beveling is not quite as automated with text or an object with rounded shapes. In these instances, a few extra steps are needed to render the bevels, but the following technique simplifies the process.

1 Type the word *Cool!* in a large, bold sans serif font. This example is shown with Futura Medium Bold at 80 point. Highlight the word. Choose Text ➢ Character Attributes. Increase the space by entering 20% in Range Kerning. You can use more or less character spacing depending on the font. Just make sure there is enough space for the bevels. Convert the text to curves. Break apart the text. Recombine the outer circles in the *o* letters with the inner circles or counters. When you finish, each letter should be a separate object.

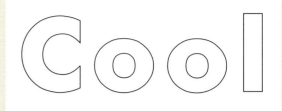

2 Select the C object. Open the Contour Roll-Up (Ctrl+F9). Change the Contour settings to Outside, Offset 0.045, and Steps 1. Press the Apply button. Separate and Ungroup the Contour. Repeat this process with each letter/object. You may need to change the Offset setting depending on the type and size of the font you use.

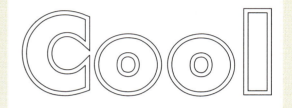

3 Add the bevels to the I object in the word, as you did with the square. With Snap To Objects on, create each bevel by using the Bezièr Tool and snapping to each series of nodes to create the bevels.

4 Apply the bevels to the two ends of the C object in the same manner as the I object and the beveled square. The rest of the C and the two o's are a little more difficult. First, let's finish the C.

5 Select the original C object. Press the Plus (+) key to make a duplicate copy. Do not make a duplicate of the contour of the letter C.

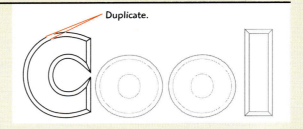

Duplicate.

6 Break apart the nodes indicated here on the duplicate of the C and the contour of the C. This can be a little tricky and confusing since there is a duplicate directly on top of the original letter C. It's a good idea to save before you attempt this and increase the number of Undo levels in Options.

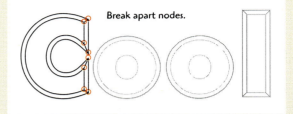

Break apart nodes.

7 Join the two sets of curves as indicated here. For clarity, the two outer sets of curves that should be joined are indicated in blue lines, and the two inner sets of curves that should be combined are indicated in green lines. Delete the lines indicated. Be careful to avoid deleting the bevels you created in step 4. You may want to marquee-select the lines you need to delete.

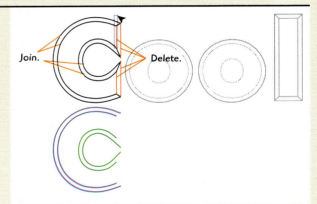

Join. Delete.

8 Select the outer curved line pair (the blue one). Marquee-select the two end nodes, as indicated. Select the Join With Segments button from the Node Edit Roll-Up. Repeat this process for the other end to close the path and create an object. To verify that the lines have now become a closed path (or an object), fill with any color fill, such as the green shown here. Repeat this process for the inner curved lines indicated in yellow.

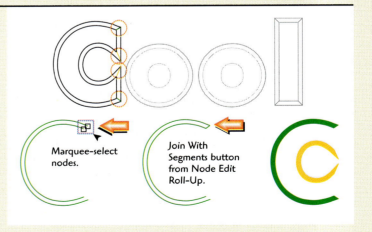

Marquee-select nodes.

Join With Segments button from Node Edit Roll-Up.

9 The o objects don't utilize the Snap To Objects technique, but the technique for adding bevels to them is still useful. Select one of the original or inner o objects. Press the Plus (+) key to create a duplicate. Break apart the inner o duplicate and the outer o contoured object. Combine the two outer ellipses and the two inner ellipses, as shown here. Repeat this process for the other o.

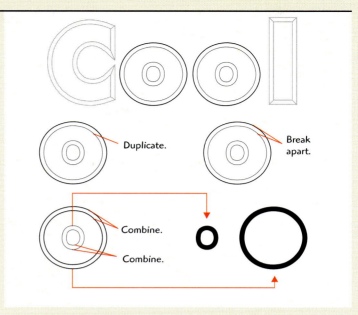

Duplicate.

Break apart.

Combine.

Combine.

HINT When you are finished creating all of the bevels, you will have some extra objects left underneath the newly created bevels—the contoured shapes that you used to build the bevels. Since the bevels are directly on top of the extra objects, it is difficult to select them. Whenever something is directly on top of something else, you can cut the top object to the clipboard (Ctrl+X), delete (not cut) or manipulate the object underneath, and then paste the top object back. When an object is cut and pasted, it is pasted in the same position from which it was cut.

10 Fill the uncurved bevels and letter objects as shown here. The curved bevels will be filled with gradient fills, so you must avoid outlines. Lines cannot be colored with gradients.

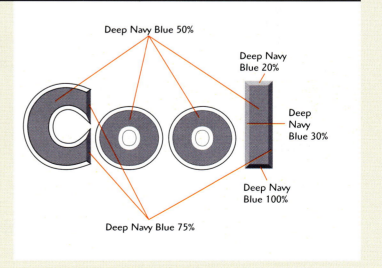

Deep Navy Blue 50%

Deep Navy Blue 20%

Deep Navy Blue 30%

Deep Navy Blue 100%

Deep Navy Blue 75%

11 To fill the curved bevels, you will have to create a custom linear gradient. Note that there are only two different kinds of gradient fills. The only difference between the two is the angle. You can fill more than one shape with a fill at a time. Select all of the shapes that need the same fill, then apply the appropriate gradient.

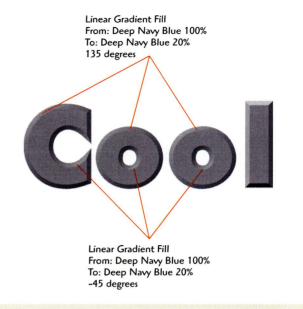

Linear Gradient Fill
From: Deep Navy Blue 100%
To: Deep Navy Blue 20%
135 degrees

Linear Gradient Fill
From: Deep Navy Blue 100%
To: Deep Navy Blue 20%
-45 degrees

TIP This technique works well for many different fonts that aren't overly complex. If you need the beveled fonts to be in a relatively small size, it is easier to create the beveled effect in a large size, then resize to the size you need.

Look! It's an organizational chart with an attitude. Automating your rendering whenever possible can increase your efficiency and help you create some useful graphics.

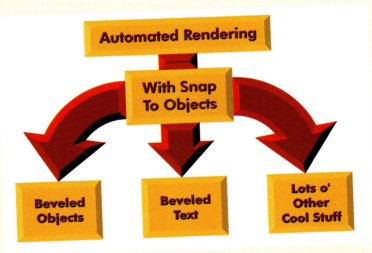

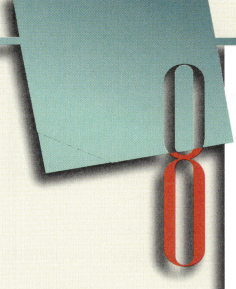

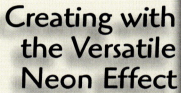

Creating with the Versatile Neon Effect

What you will learn

- Applying the neon effect to text
- Rendering pipes
- Rendering chains
- Rendering paper clips
- Rendering a chain-link fence
- Rendering spiral binding

Because it is so easy to implement, the basic neon effect has been heavily utilized (and in many instances, abused) since the dawn of vector-based graphic programs. However, it is a valuable technique that can be used to create many useful illustrations.

RADiO ACTiVE

1 Type a few words in one of your favorite fonts. Center the words. Set the type in a large point size. The font used here, Funhouse from House Industries, is set at 65 point. Fill the text with black. Once the text is the right size, Convert To Curves (Ctrl+Q).

RADiO ACTiVE

RADiO ACTiVE

2 Click on the Outline Tool button on the Toolbar. Click on the Outline Pen button in the flyout to open the Outline Pen dialog box. Change Color to Deep Yellow; Width to .035 inches; and Stretch 100%. Click on the Scale with image option. Change Corners and Line caps to rounded. Leave the rest of the options at their default settings. Click OK to close the dialog box.

3 Open the Options dialog box. Change Place duplicates and clones settings to Horizontal 0 and Vertical 0. Click on the OK button to exit Options. Duplicate the text object once by pressing Ctrl+D. Click on the Fill Tool button on the Toolbar. Click on the X button to remove the black fill. Open the Outline Pen dialog box. Change Color to White, and Width to .005 inches. Click OK.

4 Marquee-select both text objects. Select Effects ➢ Blend. The Blend defaults (20 steps) are fine, so press on the Apply button. Now you have the basic neon effect. It is the blending between two different-sized lines with contrasting colors that creates a neon effect. The bottom outline must always be thicker than the top.

Filling the top text object, instead of the bottom, with black creates a subtle, yet interesting variation. This variation highlights the fact that CorelDRAW renders an outline halfway inside and halfway outside of an object. For example, a 1-inch outline would print .5 inches inside an object and .5 inches outside. This explains why the thinner outline of the upper text object is in the center of the thicker outline of the lower text object.

Of course, you don't have to fill either of the text objects. Remove the fills from any text objects, and draw a rectangle around the text object. Be sure to send the rectangle to the back (Shift+PgDn). Fill the rectangle with a dark color such as dark purple or black. The neon effect shows up better on a dark background.

If this image doesn't thrill you, it may be because this effect has been overused in the recent past. This project is about breathing new life into the neon effect. But first, it is important to understand a few characteristics of the effect.

Understanding How the Neon Effect Works

1 Draw a 1-inch vertical line. Open the Outline Pen dialog box. Change Color to Navy Blue (40%C, 40%M, and 60%K). Change Width to .1 inches. Click OK with the line selected. Press the Plus (+) button to duplicate the line. Change the duplicate's Color to White, and Width to .01 inches, using the Outline Pen dialog box.

2 Select both lines with the Pick Tool. Blend between them with 30 steps. In the Options dialog box, change Place duplicates and clones settings to Horizontal .5 inches and Vertical 0 inches. Click OK. Duplicate the blended lines once.

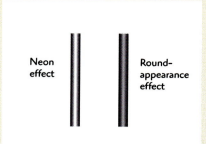

Neon effect

Round-appearance effect

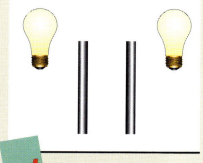

3 Carefully select the top, .01-inch white line on one of the blended lines. Simply click on the center of one of the neon lines. The Status Bar should indicate that you have a Control Curve that is an Open Path with a .01-inch Outline. If it indicates that you have a Blend Group, try again. Change the .01-inch line to 25% Navy Blue (10% C, 10% M, and 15% K).

Look carefully at each line. The line that is blended from Navy Blue to White is indicative of something

with a very close light source directly in front of it. However, the line that is blended from Navy Blue to 25% Navy Blue is indicative of something that has a light source that is farther away. The difference is fairly subtle. But, for a neon effect, you would use the more extreme contrast in the line blended from Navy Blue to White, whereas you would use the less extreme contrast in the line blended from Navy Blue to 25% Navy Blue to merely indicate that the line or object is round.

4 Another useful thing to note about the neon effect is that you can often easily move the light source. In the Options dialog box, change the Nudge option to .005 inches. Nudge the top .005-inch lines to the right or left using the right or left arrow keys. The blends will reblend. The light source will appear to be coming from the left if you nudge left, and from the right if you nudge right.

Rendering Pipes

1 Draw a 1-inch circle. Convert To Curves. Select all of the nodes with the Shape Tool. Break apart the nodes. Delete all of the segments except the lower-right segment.

2 Turn on the Snap To Objects option in the Layout menu. Draw a 1-inch line using the lower-left end of the quarter-circle segment as the beginning point. In this case, it is important for each segment to remain separate. Do not draw the line with the quarter-circle segment selected as it will cause the new line to be joined with it.

3 Select both lines. Open the Outline Pen dialog box. Change Color to 80% Black, and Width to .3 inches. Click OK. With both lines still selected, press the Plus (+) button to create duplicates. With the duplicates still selected, open the Outline Pen dialog box. Change Color to 10% Black, and Width to .025 inches.

5 Draw a .35-inch-wide by .75-inch-high rectangle. Using the Fountain Fill dialog box, fill the rectangle with a 90-degree linear gradient fill from 80% Black to 10% Black. Remove the outline from the rectangle by clicking X on the color palette with the left mouse. Center the rectangle over the intersection of the straight line and the quarter line.

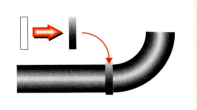

4 Select each corresponding pair of lines. Blend them separately with 40 steps.

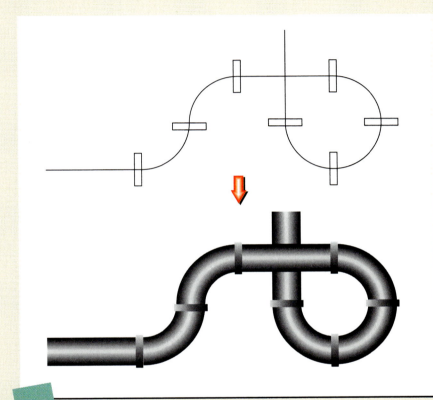

6 The straight line, the quarter-circle, and the rectangle joint are all you need to build a series of pipes. Simply duplicate the components you need, and continue adding them on. Rotate the quarter-circle segments.

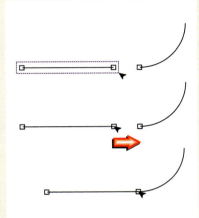

7 It is very easy to position the line segments with Snap To Objects on. Simply marquee-select both nodes in any given segment. Click and drag on the node that will connect to the corresponding node in the continuing segment. Drag the node to corresponding node. With Snap To Objects on, the node will snap right into place.

8 By nudging the lines up or down, you can make the light source move. With the curve paths, the lines will nudge out of sync, but the rectangle joints cover up the problem.

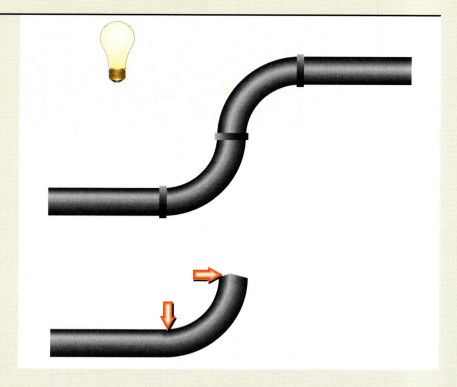

Rendering Chains

Project 7 discusses one method to render chains as a demonstration in trimming objects with holes in them. More realistic-looking chains can also be rendered using the neon effect.

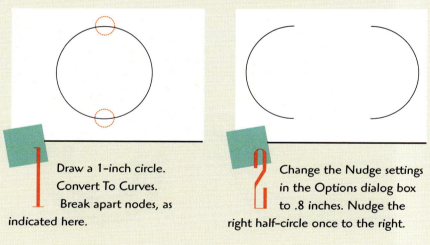

1 Draw a 1-inch circle. Convert To Curves. Break apart nodes, as indicated here.

2 Change the Nudge settings in the Options dialog box to .8 inches. Nudge the right half-circle once to the right.

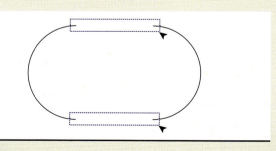

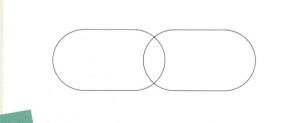

3 Shift+select both half-circles. Combine them (Ctrl+L). Open the Node Edit Roll-Up. Marquee-select the corresponding nodes at each end of the half-circles, as indicated here. Select the Join With Segments button in the Node Edit Roll-Up.

4 Open the Options dialog box. Change Place duplicates and clones settings to Horizontal 1.45 inches and Vertical 0 inches. Duplicate once.

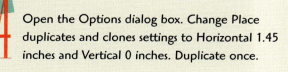

5 Break apart the nodes of the left chain link, as shown here.

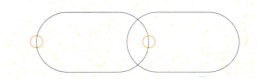

6 Open the Outline Pen dialog box. Change Color to 80% Black, and Width to .3 inches. Turn on the Scale with image option.

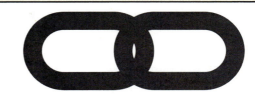

↑ Send to front.

7 Open the Scale & Mirror Roll-Up (Alt+F9). Change the Vertical setting to 75%, and leave the Horizontal setting at 100%. Press Apply.

8 Send the bottom half of the original chain to the front by selecting it and pressing Shift+PgUp.

9 Marquee-select all four of the chain segments. Press the Plus (+) button to create a duplicate. Open the Outline Pen dialog box. Change Color to 10% Black, and Width to .025 inches.

10 Shift+select each corresponding black .3-inch line and white .25-inch line. Blend between them with 50 steps.

11 Repeat this process for each corresponding pair.

Leave Place duplicates and clones set at Horizontal 1.45 inches and Vertical 0 inches. Change the Nudge settings to 1.45 inches.

Marquee-select both chains. Duplicate once. Nudge to the right once. Repeat this process as many times as necessary.

With the Scale with image option on in the Outline Pen dialog box, it is easy to resize the chains to the size you need. Downsizing is no problem; but if you increase the size, you will need more Blend steps to create the neon effect.

Rendering Paper Clips

Rendering paper clips is very similar to rendering chains.

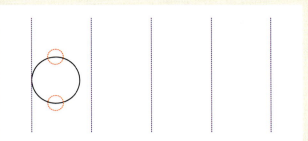

1 Position four horizontal guidelines on the page, each .625 inches apart. For instance, position guidelines at the 1-inch, 1.625-inch, 2.25-inch, and 2.875-inch horizontal positions. Turn on the Snap To Guidelines option in the Layout menu. Draw a .5-inch circle. Position it, as shown here. Convert To Curves. Break apart, as shown.

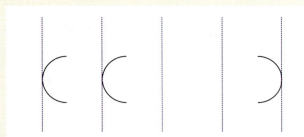

2 Ctrl+drag the right half to the rightmost guideline. Duplicate the left half with the Plus (+) button. Ctrl+drag it to the second guideline from the left, as shown.

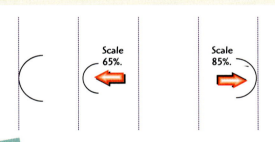

3 Scale the rightmost half-circle 85%, and the second half-circle from the left 65%, using Scale and Mirror.

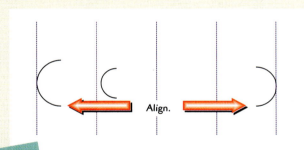

4 Ctrl+drag the right half back to the rightmost guideline. Align it with the bottom of the left half circle.

5 Ctrl+drag the second half-circle from the left to the second guideline from the left. Align the second half-circle from the left to the top of the rightmost half-circle. Select all three half-circles. Combine them.

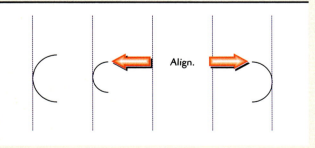

6 Open the Node Edit Roll-Up. Marquee-select the indicated node pairs with the Shape Tool. Click on the Join With Segments button. Do each pair separately.

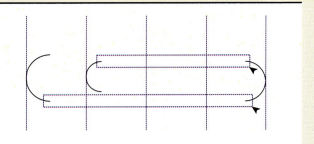

7 Turn on Snap To Objects in the Layout menu. Select the partially drawn paper-clip line. Select the Freehand Tool. Hold down the Ctrl key while drawing two separate lines between the node and guideline positions, as shown here. With the partially drawn paper-clip line selected, and using the Freehand Tool, the nodes will be automatically joined whether you start to draw the line at the guideline or at the node.

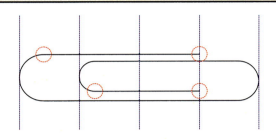

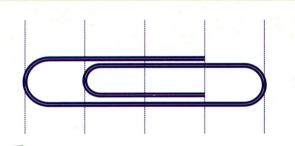

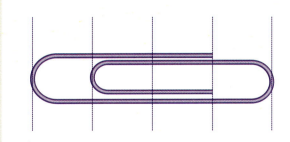

8 With the paper-clip line selected, open the Outline Pen dialog box. Change Color to Blue (100% C, 100% M). Change Width to .05 inches. Close the dialog box. Press the Plus (+) key to create a duplicate. With the duplicate selected, open the Outline Pen dialog box. Change Color to 20% Blue (20% C, 20% M). Change Width to .007 inches. Click OK.

9 With both lines selected, Blend between the two lines with 20 steps.

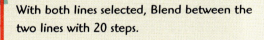

Colored paper clips are usually created with plastic sheaths that often don't cover the entire paper clip. To create this effect, simply break apart two small pieces of each end of the line. Make the thicker line slightly thinner (.4 inches in this example). Blend between a dark and light gray.

Or, of course, you can just Blend between two grays or two brass colors to create metallic paper clips. In this example, 25% M, 75% Y, 25% K were used for the darker color, and 25% M, 75% Y for the lighter color.

You can use this technique to render paper clips in all shapes and sizes.

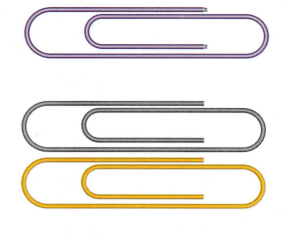

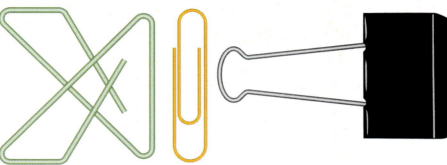

Rendering a Chain-link Fence

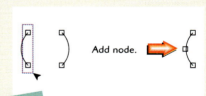

Add node.

1 There are plenty of interesting things that can be rendered utilizing the neon effect. One of the most interesting is a chain-link fence. Draw a .5-inch circle. Convert To Curves. Rotate it 45 degrees. The nodes on the circle should be positioned as shown here. Open the Node Edit Roll-Up. Select all of the nodes on the circle. Click on the Break Node button in the Node Edit Roll-Up. Select Break Apart from the Arrange menu.

2 Delete the top and bottom segments. Marquee-select both nodes on the left segment with the Shape Tool. Click once on the Add Node button on the Node Edit Roll-Up to add a node to the segment.

3 In the Options dialog box, change the Nudge option to .445 inches. Nudge the left segment to the right.

Nudge.

Break apart node.

4 With the Shape Tool, select the node that you recently added to the left segment. Select the Break Node button in the Node Edit Roll-Up. Select Break Apart from the Arrange menu. At this point, you should have three segments, as shown here.

Send to back.
Send to front.

5 Select the top-left segment. Send it To Back (Shift+PgDn), as shown. Select the bottom-left segment. Send it To Front (Shift+PgUp), as shown. This will be referred to as a link.

6 Marquee-select all three segments. In the Outline Pen dialog box, change Color to 80% Black, and Width to .05 inches.

7 Change Place duplicates and clones settings to Horizontal 1.6 inches and Vertical 0 inches. Duplicate the link twice.

8 Change Place duplicates and clones settings to Horizontal .8 inches and Vertical –1.05 inches. Marquee-select the left and middle links. Duplicate once.

9 Change the Place duplicates and clones settings to Horizontal 0 inches and Vertical –2 inches. Marquee-select all three top links. Duplicate once. In the Options dialog box, change the Nudge settings to .1 inches. Nudge the duplicate links downward once.

10 Here, we will use these links to demonstrate the chain-link-fence technique, but you can create as many as you need. Use the dimensions given here as a guide for duplicating as many links as you need.

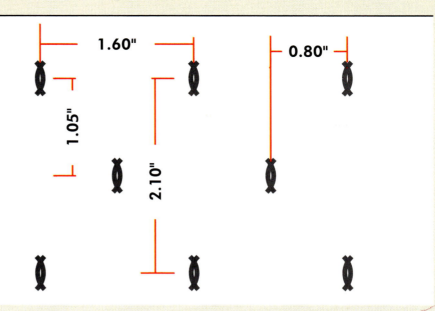

11 Turn on the Snap To Objects option in the Layout menu. Select the Freehand Tool. Draw diagonal lines between nodes as shown. Repeat this process with all corresponding nodes.

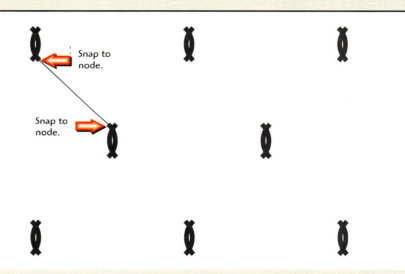

Snap to node.

Snap to node.

12 Combine (Ctrl+L) each new line with the segment that it touches. Join the nodes at each intersection point. Repeat this process for each line.

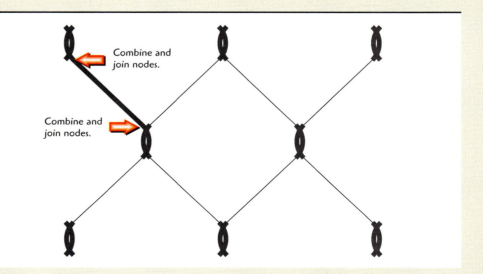

Combine and join nodes.

Combine and join nodes.

13 Select all of the lines and segments. Press the Plus (+) button. In the Outline Pen dialog box, change the duplicate's Color to 10% Black, and Width to .007 inches.

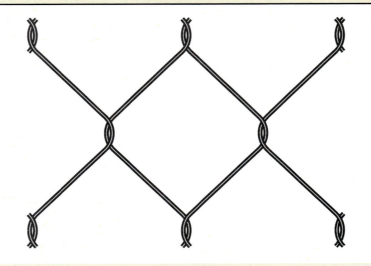

14 Before you blend each pair of lines to complete the chain–link–fence effect, you will need to look carefully at each link and make sure that it is correctly positioned. The blue circles here indicate which links are correctly positioned in this example. The red circles indicate which links are incorrectly positioned.

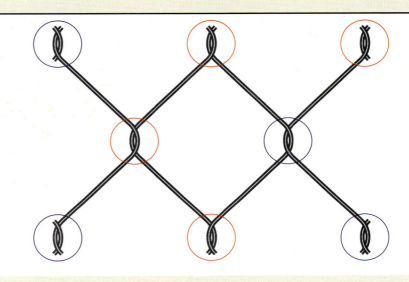

15 Correctly position each link by sending the lower–left segment to the front of each link. Repeat this process for each link until they are all positioned correctly. Start from the top and work your way down.

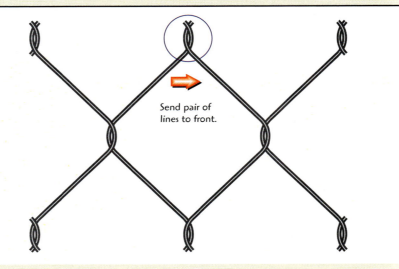

Send pair of lines to front.

16 Select corresponding pairs of lines. Blend between them with 20 steps, as shown.

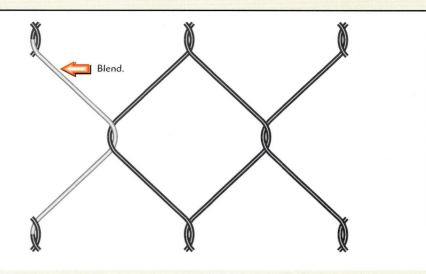

Blend.

17 Continue blending with each pair to complete the chain-link-fence effect. You can add as many links as you want.

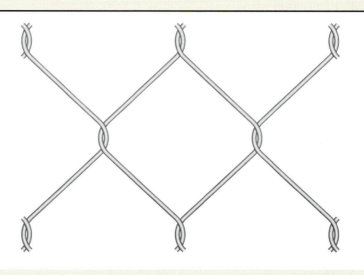

18 With the Scale with image option on in the Outline Pen dialog box, it's easy to resize the chain-link fence.

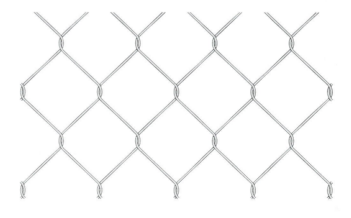

Rendering Spiral Binding

There is no rule dictating that you must blend two equal-sized lines. The following technique is useful for creating highlights.

1 Draw an ellipse .2 inches wide and 1 inch high. Convert the ellipse to curves. In the Outline Pen dialog box, change Color to 80% Black, and Width to .1 inches.

2 Press the Plus (+) button once to create a duplicate. Break apart the top and bottom nodes, as shown. Break apart the segments. Open the Outline Pen dialog box. Change Corner and Line Caps to rounded.

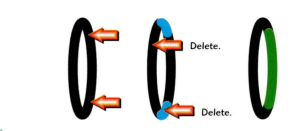

Delete.

Delete.

3 Press the Plus (+) button once to create a duplicate. Break apart the nodes, as shown. Break apart and delete the light blue segments. You should have

a line segment approximately the same as the green one here. (Note: the light blue and green colors are for illustration purposes only.)

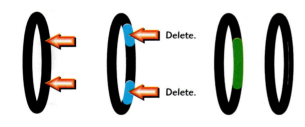

Delete.

Delete.

4 Select the newly created segment. Press the Plus (+) button once to create a duplicate. Break apart the nodes, as shown. Break apart the segments. Delete the light blue segments. You should have a line segment approxi-

mately the same as the green one here. (Again, the light blue and green colors are for illustration pur-poses only.) Select the newly created segment. Change Color to 10% Black, and Width to .003 inches.

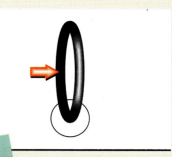

5 Select both of the smaller segments. Blend between them with 40 steps.

6 Draw a .4–inch circle around the bottom of the ellipse. Send the new circle to the back.

7 Break apart the center node on the left half-ellipse segment, as shown.

8 PowerClip the lower-left segment into the circle by choosing Effects ➤ PowerClip ➤ Place Inside Container. Point to the circle with the black arrow and click. Fill the circle with black.

9 Set Place duplicates and clones to Horizontal .75 inches and Vertical 0 inches. Click OK. Select the ellipse. Duplicate seven times.

10 Draw a 6-inch-wide by 4-inch-high rectangle. Position it, as shown. Fill the rectangle with white or with the color of your choice. Send it to the back.

11 Send all of the top-left half-ellipse segments to the back. Of course, the size of the rectangle and amount of spiral binding shown here is for demonstration purposes only. You may vary the sizes, number of spirals, and so on, to suit your purpose.

There are several different types of "spiral binding" that can be rendered with this technique. Square holes can be used instead of circular holes, the thickness of the spiral binding can vary, and true spiral binding can be rendered using the spiral techniques demonstrated in Project 2.

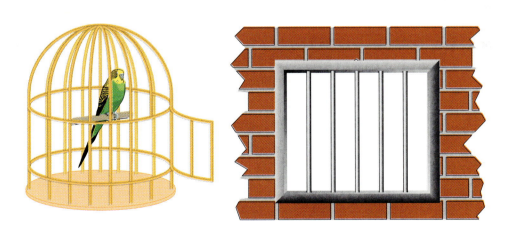

This technique has other applications. For example, you can use it to create pipe joints that look much more realistic than the blended rectangles.

There are plenty of additional things that can be rendered with the neon effect. Bars and anything else made from a thin round line can be rendered with this technique.

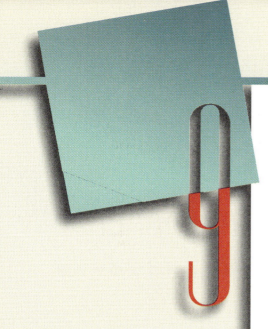

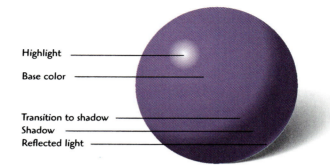

Highlight ————————————

Base color ————————————

Transition to shadow ————————————
Shadow ————————————
Reflected light ————————————

Using Custom Fountain Fills to Render Primitives

What you will learn

■ Rendering spheres, cylinders, and cones

■ Creating shiny and dull finishes

■ Moving a light source around an object

The key to transforming flat surfaces into three-dimensional curved objects is the careful placement of highlights and shading. In the printing process, highlights are rendered using a lighter tint of the image's base color by specifying a lower percentage of the cyan, magenta, yellow, and black inks. The ratio of the inks should stay constant, so a 50% tint of blue (100%C, 100%M) would be 50%C, 50%M.

Shadows are rendered by adding a percentage of black to the base color, as in 100%C, 100%M, 25%K. For primitives like spheres, cylinders, and cones, you may be tempted to use simple two-color fountain fills; but the complexities of realistic shading require the rendering of highlight, base color, transition to shadow, shadow, and reflected light. Fortunately, CorelDRAW has a custom Fountain Fill feature, allowing multiple colors to be assigned to a single fill.

These colors are used in this section.

Blue 50%C, 50%M	25%K	
Blue 10%K 50%C, 50%M, 10%K	50%K	Red 100%M, 100%Y
Blue 30%K 50%C, 50%M, 30%K	60%K	Red 10%K 100%M, 100%Y, 10%K
50% Blue 25%C, 25%M	70%K	Red 35%K 100%M, 100%Y, 35%K
White	80%K	50% Red 50%M, 50%Y

Rendering Spheres

1 The first subject is a ball with a matte finish, and a light source from the upper left. The base color of the ball is Blue (50%C, 50%M). Draw a circle. With the circle selected, press F11 to bring up the Fountain Fill dialog box. Select Radial as the Type. Choose the Custom option. Assign the following colors to the positions indicated by double-clicking within the custom blend preview window, then entering the correct value in the Position dialog: Position 0%: Blue 10%K; Position 20%: Blue 10%K; Position 25%: Blue 30%K;

Position 40%: Blue 30%K; Position 50%: Blue 10%K; Position 65%: Blue; Position 100%: 50% Blue. For the light source from the upper left, set the Horizontal and Vertical Center offsets to 20. The color values and positions are given as a guide only, so feel free to experiment.

2 To render a shiny ball, start from the Fountain Fill options used before, and simply change the 65% position marker to 90%, and the 100% position color to White.

HINT
For an explanation of how to create different types of shadows, see Project 16.

HINT
While a dull finish is characterized by a gradual transition to a soft highlight, the shiny ball shown in step 2 has an abrupt transition to an intense glare highlight.

3 To move the light source around, change the Center offset values in the Fountain Fill dialog box. For a light source from the top center, set Horizontal Center offset to 0, and Vertical Center offset to −20.

HINT

For future use, you can save these fills as Presets in the Fountain Fill dialog box by entering a new name in the Presets box and pressing the Plus (+) button. Or you can save them as Styles by selecting the ball with the right mouse button, clicking on Styles, then Save Style Properties, entering a new name, and making sure Fill is checked, then clicking OK.

4 To add a feature of a different color, select the original circle and duplicate. (Use the Plus [+] key on the numeric keypad to duplicate without moving.) Change the colors of the duplicate to those appropriate for a red sphere. In Tools ➢ Options dialog box, make sure Automatically center new powerclip contents is turned off. PowerClip the red circle into the stripe by choosing Effects ➢ PowerClip ➢ Place Inside Container. The highlight and shadow areas will now match perfectly. This same technique will work for the cylinder and cone examples that follow.

HINT

When putting a stripe or other feature of a different color on the ball, if you just apply the same fill, the highlight and shading won't match.

Highlight mismatch.

Rendering Cylinders

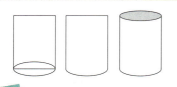

1 To draw a cylinder, first align an ellipse and a rectangle as shown. (Snap To Objects will help here.) Select the rectangle. Weld by selecting Arrange ➢ Weld to bring up the Weld Roll-Up. Then, click on Weld To, point to the ellipse, and click. Draw another ellipse and place it on top.

2 For simplicity, the base color of the cylinder is 50%K, and the light source is from the front. In the Fountain Fill dialog (F11), select Linear as the Type, and Angle: 0. Choose the Custom option. Assign the following colors: Position 0%: 70%K; Position 50%: 25%K; Position 100%: 70%K. The elliptical top is filled with a Two Color Linear Fountain Fill; Angle: 90; From: 25%K; To: 50%K.

As the light source is moved around to the left, the right part of the cylinder falls into shadow. The shading crests to the shadow, then holds relatively constant. The far right side of the cylinder shows reflected light. The source could be a nearby wall, but this rendering technique is so prevalent that it is frequently used even when an obvious source is not in the scene.

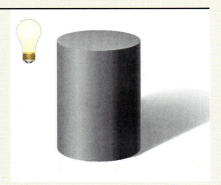

3 With the light source at the upper left, assign the following colors: Position 0%: 50K; Position 25%: 25%K; Position 50%: 50%K; Position 65%: 60%K; Position 75%: 80%K; Position 95%: 80%K; Position 100%: 60%K. The top is filled with the same fountain fill as in the previous step, except the angle is changed to 81.

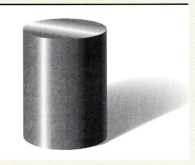

4 For a shiny cylinder, change the 25% position to white. Add colors at the 15% and 35% positions, assigning both 40%K. The top is filled with a Custom Linear Fountain Fill: Angle: 81; Edge pad: 25; Position 0%: 50%K, Position 50%: White, Position 100%: 50%K.

Rendering Cones

1 Conical fountain fills work great for (you guessed it) shading cones. To draw an outline of a cone as viewed from a slightly elevated angle, overlap a triangle and an ellipse, as shown. Select both. Weld.

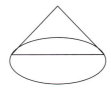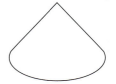

2 This first example is rendered in red, with a matte finish, and a centered light source. In the Fountain Fill dialog, select Conical as the Type; set Angle to 90; Horizontal Center offset to 0, and Vertical Center offset to 50. Choose the Custom option. Assign the following colors: Position 0%: 50% Red; Position 25%: Red; Position 100%: Red.

It may not be obvious why the 25% position was chosen, but there's a trick shown in the next steps that will help you visualize what's happening.

3 Here the light source has been moved to the upper left. You could just start playing around with the position settings in the Fountain Fill dialog, but it helps to apply the fill to a rectangle placed behind the cone, make adjustments, and then copy the fill to the cone. With Snap To Objects on in the Layout menu, snap guidelines to the nodes on the cone. Turn on Snap To Guidelines. Draw a rectangle behind the cone. (Give the

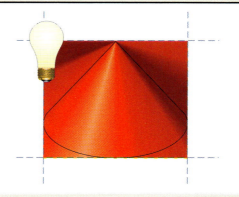

cone an outline, but no fill.) Apply a conical fill to the rectangle complete with shadow and highlight colors. It's

easy to see where adjustments are needed. In the example here, the shadow is way off the cone.

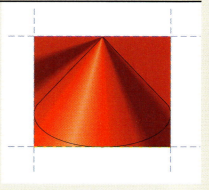

> **HINT**
>
> While the settings in step 4 worked for this cone, they cannot be applied universally. Tall skinny cones will need different settings than those required for short fat cones.

4 Move the position markers to put the shadow on the right side of the cone, and squeeze in a zone of reflected light right at the edge. The following settings were used here: Angle: 75; Position 0%: 50% Red; Position 9%: Red; Position 18%: Red 10%K; Position 22%: Red 35%K; Position 29%: Red 35%K; Position 33%: Red 10%K; Position 100%: Red 10%K.

5 In Edit ➤ Copy Properties From, click OK. Check Fill. Click on the rectangle. Delete the rectangle.

6 By assigning White to the 0% Position, and moving the 9% Position in to 6%, the cone takes on a shiny appearance.

10

Using Highlights and Shading to Render Form

What you will learn

- Rendering form
- Using blends to create realistic highlights and shading

An artist is frequently presented with the problem of giving form to a uniformly colored object. Of course, color only exists where there is light, which creates the shading and highlights that mold a two-dimensional representation into a three-dimensional object. The Blend feature is a powerful tool for rendering these different tonal values. Begin by creating an outline of the object, in this case the chocolate candy. Fill with the object's base color. For each highlight and shadow, create a beginning shape filled with the base color. Then duplicate, reshape, and change the tonal value to one suitable for a highlight or shadow. Blend between the two.

HINT

When you're first starting out, it helps to set up and light the subject of your illustration to use as a reference for placing the highlights and shading. Photographs can also be a big help. As you become more adept at rendering form, a process of logical lighting can be applied, drawing on your knowledge to place the highlights and shading where they would best convey the shape of the object. Since most objects can be thought of as being constructed from primitive shapes, Project 9 on rendering primitives is a good place to start gaining this knowledge.

These colors are used in this section.

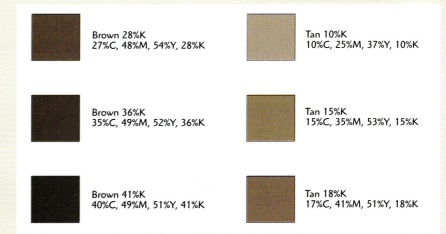

Brown 28%K
27%C, 48%M, 54%Y, 28%K

Tan 10%K
10%C, 25%M, 37%Y, 10%K

Brown 36%K
35%C, 49%M, 52%Y, 36%K

Tan 15%K
15%C, 35%M, 53%Y, 15%K

Brown 41%K
40%C, 49%M, 51%Y, 41%K

Tan 18%K
17%C, 41%M, 51%Y, 18%K

1 Begin by drawing an outline of the subject. While you can apply this technique to any uniformly colored object, this example uses a piece of chocolate candy. Fill the outline with the base color of the object, here Brown 28%K.

2 Create an area of dark shading to help define the center ridge of chocolate. First, draw the shape (outlined in blue for clarity only). Then, fill to the background color. Duplicate (Plus [+] key on the numeric keypad). Use the Shape Tool to node edit to the red outlined shape. Fill to Brown 41%K. Select both. Blend using Ctrl+B to bring up the Blend Roll-Up.

HINT

The harshness or softness of the highlight or shading can be controlled by the spacing between the blend from and blend to shapes, while the intensity is controlled by the color values of the two blends.

HINT

When creating an illustration with a lot of blends such as this one, you may find it expedient to restrict the number of Blend steps to five or so during the roughing-in stage. This significantly reduces screen redraw times. When you're ready to apply the finishing touches, simply select each blend object in turn, change the number of Blend steps to an appropriate number using the Blend Roll-Up, and Apply the new values.

3 Next create a highlight at the base of the opposite ridge. Proceed as in step 2, creating a base-colored object, duplicating, then reshaping, only this time fill the reshaped object to Tan 15%K.

4 Create a more intense highlight at the top of the same ridge, using a fill of Tan 10%K.

5 Draw this dark sliver to define where the chocolate curls over the top, using a fill for the "blend to" object of Brown 36%K.

HINT Here are outlines for all the blend objects—red for highlights and blue for shading.

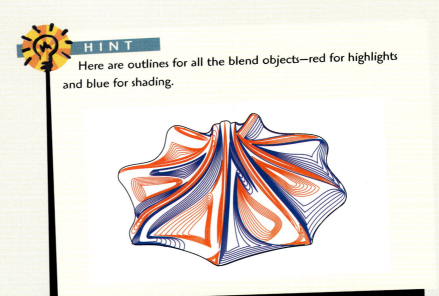

6 Finally, create this triangular-shaped highlight using a fill of Tan 18%K. The concave shape of one segment of the candy is now complete.

7 Continue to build up areas of highlight and shading. The form of the candy will slowly emerge.

8 The finished illustration with all the highlights and shading added looks good enough to eat.

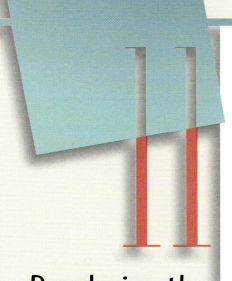

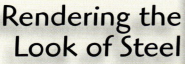

Rendering the
Look of Steel

What you will learn

- Rendering flat
  steel surfaces

- Creating steel cylinders

- Using rectangles for
  efficient construction

The appearance of metal is characterized by abrupt gradations between
light and dark. Curved shapes in particular are rendered using several
alternating bands. The bolt in this
exercise is constructed from simple
shapes. With options for Edge pad
and multiple colors, CorelDRAW's
fountain fills do all the work.

These colors are used in this section.
If you're working in grayscale, you
can use the black values only. With
four-color printing, the small percentages of cyan and magenta will
give a slight blue-gray tint typical of
steel.

	Steel 5%K 3%C, 2%M, 5%K		
	Steel 10%K 3%C, 2%M, 10%K		Steel 50%K 10%C, 5%M, 50%K
	Steel 25%K 10%C, 5%M, 25%K		Steel 75%K 10%C, 5%M, 75%K
	White		Steel 100%K 10%C, 5%M, 100%K

Drawing the Bolt Head

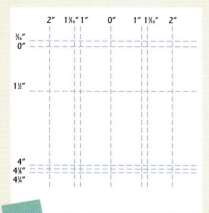

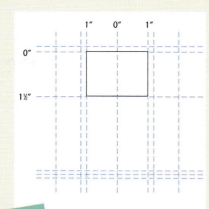

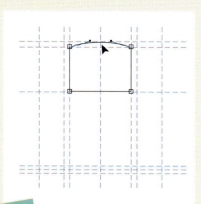

1 In Layout ➤ Grid and Ruler Setup ➤ Grid tab, set the Grid Frequency to 16 per inch in both the Horizontal and Vertical settings. In Layout, turn on Snap To Grid and Snap To Objects. Pull in the ruler zero point near the top of your page, centered left to right. Pull in guidelines, as indicated.

2 Snap a rectangle to the guidelines, as shown. Convert To Curves (Ctrl+Q).

3 With the Shape Tool, double-click on the top line to bring up the Node Edit Roll-Up. Select the Curve Node button. With Snap To Guidelines and Snap To Objects off for this step only, click and drag from the center of the line straight up so that the curve almost touches the guideline above.

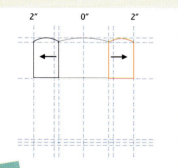

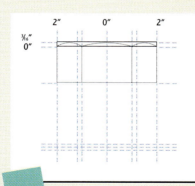

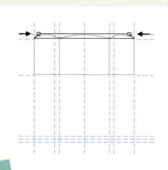

4 With the Pick Tool, stretch and duplicate by dragging the right-middle handle straight left until it aligns with the left 2-inch guide. Click the right mouse button to leave the original (black outline for clarity). Repeat the process, using the left handle and dragging to the right (red outline for clarity).

5 Snap a rectangle to the guidelines, as shown.

6 Convert To Curves. With the Shape Tool, select the top two nodes. In the Node Edit Roll-Up, use the Stretch and Scale option and Shift+drag toward the middle until the Status Line reads about 90%.

7 Fill the objects, as shown. Send the trapezoid-shaped object To Back. Add the two white-line highlights, using about a .5-point line width for this size bolt.

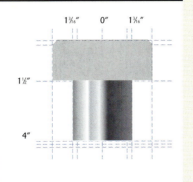

Radial Fountain Fill
Horizontal Offset: -25%
Vertical Offset: -50%
From: Steel 75%K
To: White

Line highlights

Linear Fountain Fills:
Angle: 45
Edge Pad: 30
From: Steel 50%K
To: Steel 5%K

Angle: 135
Edge Pad: 25
From: Steel 50%K
To: White

Angle: -135
Edge Pad: 20
From: Steel 75%K
To: Steel 25%K

Drawing the Shaft and Threads

1 Draw the rectangle shown. Fill with a Custom Linear Fountain Fill using the following settings: Angle: 0; Position 0%: Steel 50%K; Position 25%: White; Position 30%: Steel 25%K; Position 45%: Steel 5%K; Position 60%: Steel 75%K; Position 100%: Steel 50%K. (Bolt head shown in gray for reference only.)

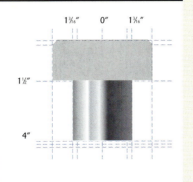

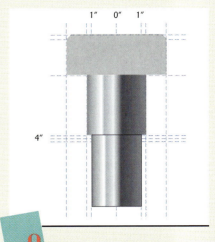

2 Draw another rectangle as shown, extending as far down as the length of the bolt. Select Edit ➢ Copy Properties From. Check Outline Pen, Outline Color, and Fill. Click OK. Then, click on the rectangle from the previous step.

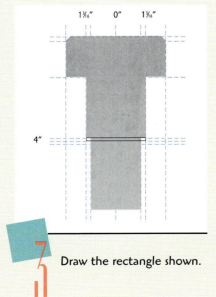

3 Draw the rectangle shown.

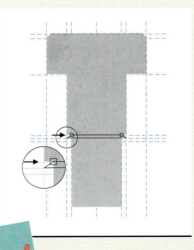

4 Convert To Curves. With the Shape Tool, snap the top two nodes to the guideline intersections, as shown.

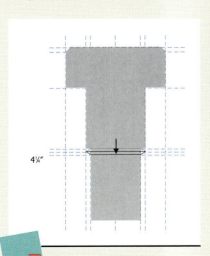

5 Drag the top-middle handle straight down to the next horizontal guideline. Click the right mouse button to leave the original.

98   PROJECT **11** RENDERING THE LOOK OF STEEL

6 Select both trapezoids. Click on them again to bring up the skew and rotate handles. Drag the right skew handle up until the peak of the thread on the left side is vertically aligned with the root of the thread on the right side.

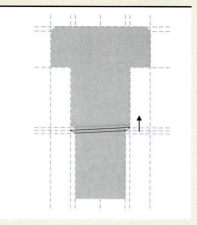

7 Fill the top trapezoid to Steel 50%K. Send To Back. (Outline for clarity only.) Fill the bottom trapezoid to Steel 75%K.

8 Select the two trapezoids. Select Arrange ➢ Transform ➢ Position. Enter –.25 Vertical. Press Apply To Duplicate.

9 Repeat until the entire threaded portion is full.

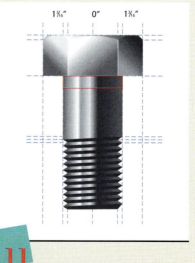

10 Convert the rectangle to curves. With Snap To Objects on, use the Shape Tool to snap the highlighted nodes on the outlined objects, as shown.

11 Draw the rectangle shown.

12 Use the same technique as before to curve the bottom section of the shadow (step 3 in the Drawing the Bolt Head section). To darken the shadow, choose Effects ➢ Lens. Then select Color Limit from the List box, set Rate: 25; Color: Black.

HINT

The Lens feature was introduced in CorelDRAW 5. Version 4 users can assign the same basic fountain fill as the underlying shaft, only add 25%K to each color value.

13 Screws with different diameter sizes may be constructed by starting back at the beginning of the Drawing the Shaft and Threads section. Simply stretching the already-completed bolt will cause the threads to look too deep or shallow.

A rounded screw head is better made by knife-cutting an ellipse in half. To draw the screwdriver slot, overlap a rectangle and trim (Arrange ➢ Trim). Use a radial fountain fill for the shading.

14 Tapered shafts can be constructed from the standard shaft by using CorelDRAW's Envelope Editing feature (Effects ➢ Envelope, or Ctrl+F7).

Even though the shapes will be tapered, the fountain fills will still be linear. One solution to this is to use DRAW's Adobe Illustrator export and import filters. Exporting in Adobe Illustrator format will convert the fountain fills to many individual objects, each a slightly different shade. (The imported version looks identical to the original; however, should you want to change colors later, this is an extremely complex editing job. Make sure you have a copy of the original saved.) These objects will appropriately distort when the Envelope feature is used. The edited shaft, in this case, appears to be filled with a "tapered" fountain fill.

VARIATION

A brass bolt can be rendered starting with a basic brass color of 25%M, 75%Y. To render the different metal colorations, build tint values by taking percentages of the basic magenta and yellow values. Build shade values by adding varying percentages of black.

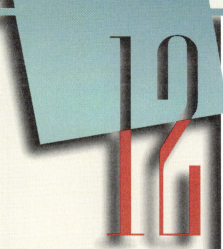

12

Drawing Symmetrical Objects

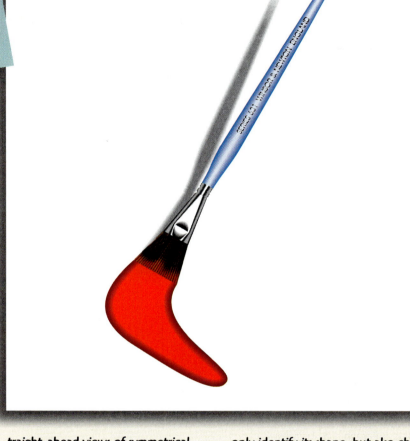

What you will learn

■ Mastering object-construction techniques

■ Shading symmetrical objects

■ Rendering shiny metal

Straight-ahead views of symmetrical objects are easy to construct, as they are usually built from simple geometric shapes. For a three-dimensional look, highlight and shadow areas are needed. Central highlights, like the ones on the brush, readily identify the shape of the object. Shiny metal is characterized by abrupt changes from light to dark. The highlights on the ferrule of the paintbrush not only identify its shape, but also characterize its surface.

The second exercise, the creation of a chess piece, shows how to deal with angled and sharply curved sections. Objects drawn this way easily convey the maximum information to the viewer. Use this method for technical and informational drawings, as well as eye-catching designs.

These colors are used in the brush exercise. The chess piece exercise uses grayscale values in 10% increments from 10%K to 100%K.

Blue
100%C, 40%M

20%Blue
20%C, 8%M

Brown 10%K
35%M, 75%Y, 10%K

White

Brown 50%K
50%M, 50%Y, 50%K

20%K

Brown 65%K
50%M, 50%Y, 65%K

70%K

Black

Using Symmetrical Construction Techniques to Render Shiny and Metallic Surfaces

1 Draw one side of the brush handle. For this simple shape you need only four nodes.

2 Using the Scale & Mirror page of the Transform Roll-Up, Mirror horizontally. Click the top-right anchor point. Apply To Duplicate.

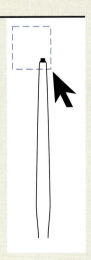

3 Select both sides. Combine. Use the Shape Tool to marquee-select the intersecting points. Choose Join Nodes in the Node Edit Roll-Up.

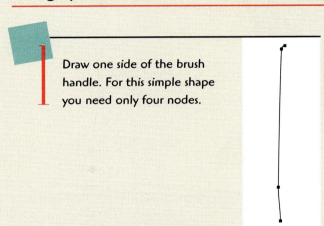

4 With the object still active, select the highlighted nodes. Click the Join With Segment button in the Node Edit Roll-Up.

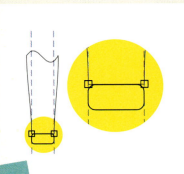
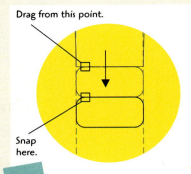
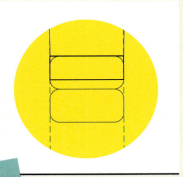

5 With Snap To Guidelines and Snap To Objects on, snap guidelines to the points shown. Draw the rectangle. Use the Shape Tool to round the corners.

6 With the Pick Tool, drag the rounded rectangle down from the highlighted point. Click the right mouse button to leave a copy. Snap to the point shown on the original rectangle.

7 The top rectangle needs to have rounded corners on the bottom and sharp corners on the top. Add the rectangle shown. With it active, Shift+select the rounded rectangle and . . .

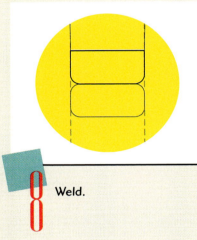
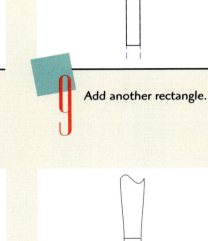
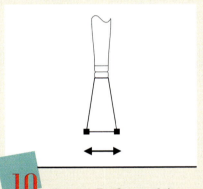

8 Weld.

9 Add another rectangle.

10 Convert To Curves. Select the two bottom nodes. Choose the Stretch and Scale Nodes button in the Node Edit Roll-Up. Shift+drag to get the trapezoid shape.

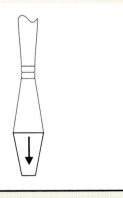
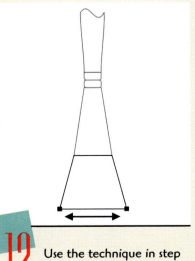

11 With the trapezoid selected, use the Pick Tool to drag the top-middle handle straight down. Click the right mouse button to leave a copy.

12 Use the technique in step 10 to stretch the bottom two nodes, as shown.

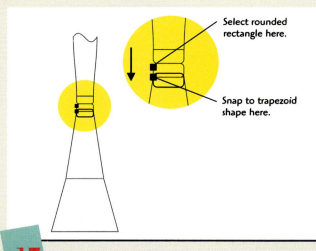

Select rounded
rectangle here.

Snap to trapezoid
shape here.

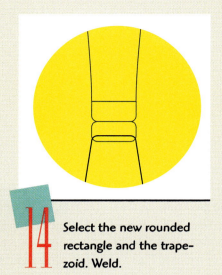

13 With the Pick Tool, select the lower rounded rectangle at the highlighted node. Drag straight down to the point indicated (top-left node on the trapezoid). Click the right mouse button to leave a copy.

14 Select the new rounded rectangle and the trapezoid. Weld.

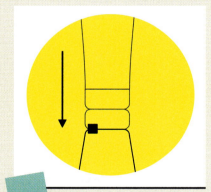

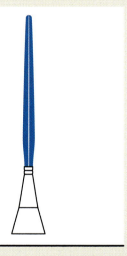

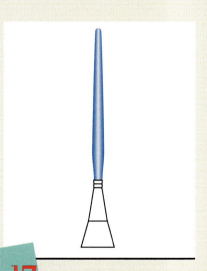

15 With the newly welded shape still active, stretch it smaller by snapping the top-middle handle to the point shown.

16 Color the brush handle Blue. In the Scale & Mirror page of the Transform Roll-Up, Scale horizontally to 10%. Apply To Duplicate. Fill to 20% Blue.

17 Select the two handle shapes. Blend.

HINT

You can snap a handle to a point that is not in line with the handle by clicking the handle and dragging diagonally. If you're moving a middle handle, the object will stretch in one direction only.

18 Select the top metal shape. Shift+drag one of the middle side handles to stretch horizontally. Click the right mouse button to leave the original.

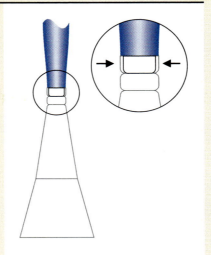

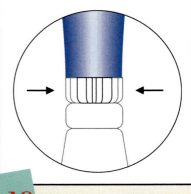

19 Repeat Stretch until you have five objects total.

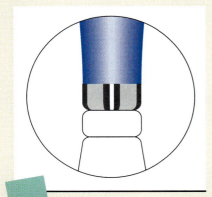

20 From the outside in, fill to 70%K, 20%K, 20%K, 70%K, and White.

21 From the outside in again, Blend the objects: 70%K to 20%K, 20%K to 70%K, and 70%K to White.

HINT

To create compound blends, select the two outer objects. Blend. Click off the blend to deselect. Zoom in and carefully select the inner object of the blend you just created. The Status Line will identify it as a Control Curve. Shift+click the next inner object. Blend the two.

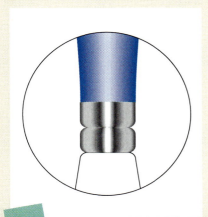

22 Repeat steps 18 through 21 for the rounded rectangle.

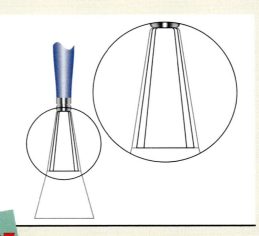

23 Create the two new shapes, as in step 18.

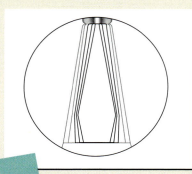

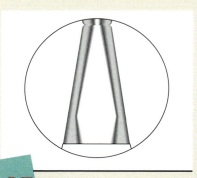

24 Add the additional objects. It's easiest to copy the original trapezoid; add two control points where the tuck occurs. Use the Stretch and Scale Nodes option in the Node Edit Roll-Up to manipulate to the final shapes.

25 Fill these shapes with the same colors as in step 20. Blend, as in step 21.

26 Draw an ellipse. Use the Knife Tool (found on the Shape Tool flyout) to cut at the two side nodes. Use the Join With Segment button in the Node Edit Roll-Up to close each half. Optionally, check Automatically Close Objects in Knife Tool Properties. (Note: users with versions prior to 6, see the section on the Knife Tool in the Introduction.)

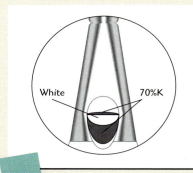

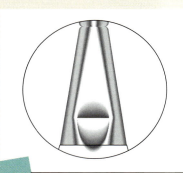

27 Fill the top shape to White. Drag the middle-bottom handle of the bottom shape straight down to elongate. Fill to 70%K.

28 Duplicate and stretch (once for the top shape, twice for the bottom), filling as shown.

29 Blend, using a simple blend for the top two objects. The bottom three objects will need a compound blend, as in step 21.

30 Fill the brushes with Brown 65%K. Move To Front.

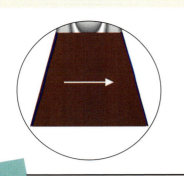

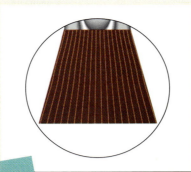

31 Draw a brush hair about .5-point line width, depending on final image size, Brown 50%K (but shown in blue for clarity). Mirror horizontally. Apply To Duplicate. Drag straight right.

32 Blend in 16 steps.

33 Add more brush hairs using different colors. (For example, try Brown 10%K for one blend, and Black for another).

Rendering a Chess Piece with Angled Sections and Different Lighting

The brush contour was relatively simple, whereas objects with lots of sharp angles, like this chess piece, are more complex to realistically shade. If you blend the whole shape, you'll get the result shown at the far right.

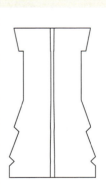

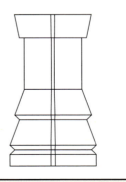

1 You'll need to create each section individually.

2 Select all the pieces. In the Scale & Mirror Page of the Transform Roll-Up, Scale horizontally to about 5% or so. Apply To Duplicate.

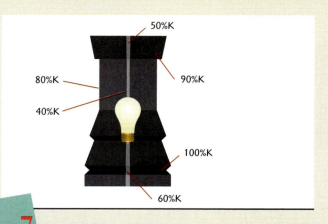

For a centrally located light source, fill as shown.

3

Blend each pair.

4

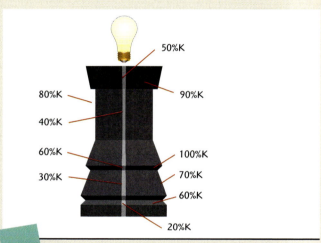

With the light source centered horizontally but above the object, the upward-facing sections are rendered lightest, and downward-facing sections are rendered darkest.

5

Here's the result when all the blends are complete. Look closely at the bottom notch for this step and step 4 to see the change.

6

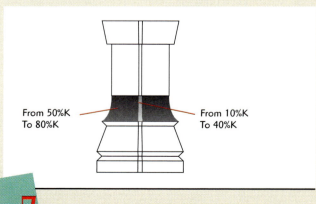

From 50%K To 80%K   From 10%K To 40%K

Curved sections are rendered using two objects filled with Linear Fountain Fills.

7

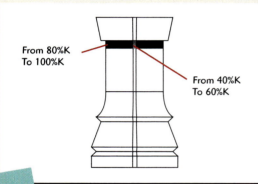

8 Here's the result when the two objects from the previous step are blended and placed into the previously completed piece.

HINT
Blending fountain fills will significantly increase screen redraw and print times. When using this technique, try to keep the objects small and shapes simple. Stay away from angles that are not multiples of 90 degrees.

From 80%K
To 100%K

From 40%K
To 60%K

9 A soft shadow is created in a similar manner as the curved section. Start with two objects filled with Linear Fountain Fills.

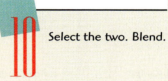

10 Select the two. Blend.

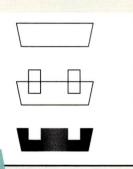

11 To add notches to the top of the piece, Duplicate the original "blend from" shape. Overlap two rectangles, and Trim. Align over the original. Select the original blend. PowerClip into the notched object.

HINT
When using the PowerClip feature, sometimes the object you want to PowerClip into (i.e., the container) is obscured by the container's contents. If all objects reside on the same layer, select the contents and press Shift+PgDn (send To Back). The screen will redraw, the contents will still be selected, and the container is now available to be selected. Choose Place Inside Container. Click the container object.

13 CHISEL

Chiseling Text

What you will learn

- Creating object centerlines

- Shading straight and curved sections

- Rendering shiny surfaces

Realistic three-dimensional chiseled text is a stunning effect, but you'll have to work to get it. The first step is to segment the letter forms into closed objects that abut along the center of the letter outline. A slick way to get the necessary centerline is to blend opposing outlines in one step. Oftentimes this trick will do all the work for you. Sometimes it just gets you close.

The first part of this project will look at how to segment some representative letter forms, and at some of the problems you might encounter. The next step is to fill the shapes with solid, fountain, or blended object fills so that the shading is consistent with the light source. In preparation for that, basic principles of shading will be discussed. Finally, these shading principles will be applied to some sample letter forms.

These colors are used in this section.

50% Red 50%M, 50%Y	Red 25%K 100%M, 100%Y, 25%K
Red 100%M, 100%Y	60% Red 60%M, 60%Y	Red 35%K 100%M, 100%Y, 35%K
10% Red 10%M, 10%Y	70% Red 70%M, 70%Y	Red 40%K 100%M, 100%Y, 40%K
20% Red 20%M, 20%Y	80% Red 80%M, 80%Y	Red 50%K 100%M, 100%Y, 50%K
30% Red 30%M, 30%Y	Red 5%K 100%M, 100%Y, 5%K	Red 60%K 100%M, 100%Y, 60%K
40% Red 40%M, 40%Y	Red 15%K 100%M, 100%Y, 15%K	Red 75%K 100%M, 100%Y, 75%K

Segmenting Curved Letters

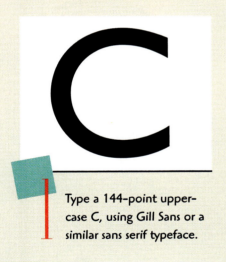

1 Type a 144-point upper-case C, using Gill Sans or a similar sans serif typeface.

2 Use the Knife Tool (found on the Shape Tool flyout) to cut at the highlighted nodes. Under View ➤ Properties ➤ Tools, make sure that Leave as one object and Automatically close object options are turned off in the Knife Tool Properties dialog box. As a shortcut, double-clicking on the Knife Tool button will bring up this dialog box. (Note: users with CorelDRAW versions prior to 6, see the Knife Tool section in the Introduction.)

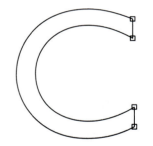

If you select the two (red) lines and Blend in one step, you get this—the result of blending two lines created in the opposite direction. The node mapping option in the Blend Roll-Up is used to fix this.

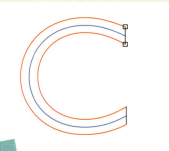

3 Select the two lines shown in red with the Pick Tool. In the Blend Roll-Up, enter a value of 1 Step. Click the Speedometer tab, then click Map Nodes. Click the curved arrow on one of the highlighted nodes, then on the other. Click Apply. (Lines shown in blue and red for clarity only.)

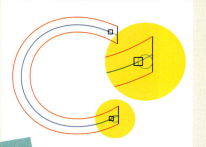

4 Separate. Click away from any object to deselect. Then reselect the (blue) blend object. Ungroup. The center-line will need to be shortened at both ends to add the triangular bevels later. If you want, use a 6-point-diameter circle as a guide. Then click at the appropriate location with the Knife Tool.

5 Delete the two small line sections. Duplicate the middle line (Plus [+] key on the numeric key pad). Shift+select the inner line. Combine. Close, using the Join With Segment button in the Node Edit Roll-Up to add the two straight lines. Send Back One.

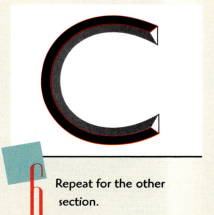

6 Repeat for the other section.

7 With Snap To Objects on, use the Beziér tool to draw the triangular end shapes, snapping to the nodes on the existing curves.

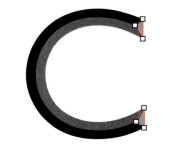

Segmenting Straight Letters

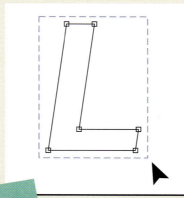

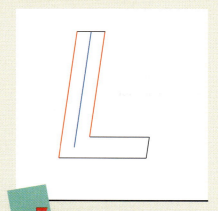

1 Type a 144-point upper-case L, using a sans serif typeface. (Gill Sans Bold Italic was used here.) Convert To Curves.

2 With the Shape Tool, marquee-select all the nodes. In the Node Edit Roll-Up, click the Break Node button. Break apart.

3 Select the two (red) lines. Blend in one step. To get the desired result, you'll have to map nodes as in step 3 in the previous exercise.

4 Blend the other two lines as shown.

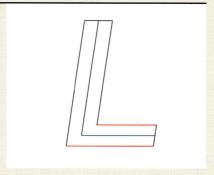

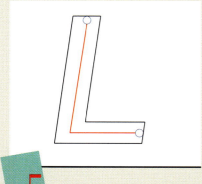

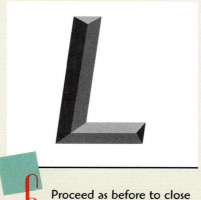

5 Use the 6-point circle as a guide to shorten the lines.

6 Proceed as before to close the shapes as in steps 5 through 7 of the Segmenting Curved Letters exercise.

Working with Compound Shapes

HINT

You don't need to convert an object to curves to use the Knife Tool, but doing so and then breaking apart allows you to see where the existing nodes are.

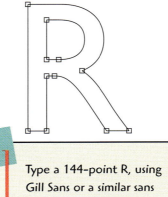

1 Type a 144-point R, using Gill Sans or a similar sans serif typeface. Knife at the highlighted nodes as in step 2 of the Segmenting Curved Letters exercise.

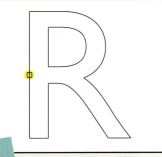

2 Cut the outline at a location that does not have an existing node. Use the Knife Tool again.

3 Blend all the opposing lines, as shown here. Separate and Ungroup as in step 4 of the Segmenting Curved Letters exercise.

4 With Snap To Objects on, drag the nodes on top of each other until it looks like the example here.

5 You'll need to fine-tune the shape under the highlighted area by dragging control points until the spacing between the centerline and the letter outline looks even.

HINT

Here, your artistic eye comes into play. The highlighted area still is not quite right in Step 4, and the software can't automatically fix it for you. You'll have to zoom in and manually drag control points.

6 Close and fill the shapes as in steps 4 through 7 in the Segmenting Curved Letters exercise.

Tricky Stuff

S

1 Type a 144-point upper-case S in Times New Roman PS or in a similar typeface. Convert To Curves.

HINT

If you proceed as before and Blend the two red lines, you get the image on the left. Why? Because each line has an extra node at a location where there is no corresponding node on the other line (right image). To remedy this, additional nodes will need to be added, and then the lines reblended, as in Step 2. (Different typefaces will present similar problems, but the locations of the missing nodes will vary.)

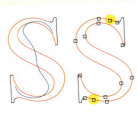

2 Use the Knife Tool as in step 2 in the Segmenting Curved Letters exercise to separate the two sides of the letter form. With the Shape Tool, click on the line at the highlighted locations. In the Node Edit Roll-Up, click the + icon (Add Node button).

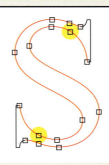

3 Proceed as in step 3 in the Segmenting Curved Letters exercise, using the Blend Roll-Up and the Map Nodes button to Blend in one step.

4 Proceed as in step 5 in the Working with Compound Shapes exercise, and steps 5 through 7 in the Segmenting Curved Letters exercise. Typefaces like this need three triangular-shaped bevels at the serifs.

HINT

Lowercase letters and fancy typefaces are particularly tricky. Here are the closed shapes for a lowercase g to help you see the techniques you've learned in this project.

Shading Principles

HINT

The illustrations in steps 1 and 2 in this exercise demonstrate that there is a strong conditioning to expect the light source from the upper left. Consequently, illustrations rendered with this light direction are the most easily interpreted.

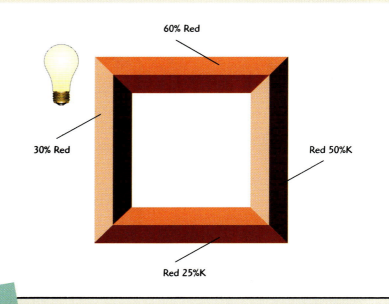

60% Red

30% Red

Red 50%K

Red 25%K

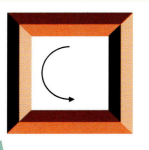

1 A square with the segments shaded as above appears to protrude from the background. (Note that the inner segments use the same colors as the outer ones, but on the opposite side.)

2 Rotate 180 degrees. The square appears to be chiseled into the surface.

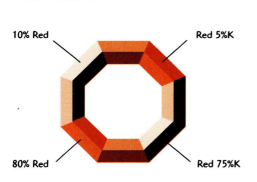

10% Red

Red 5%K

80% Red

Red 75%K

Custom Radial Fountain Fill
Horizontal: –38%
Vertical: 15%
From: Red 60%K
To: 20% Red
50% position: Red

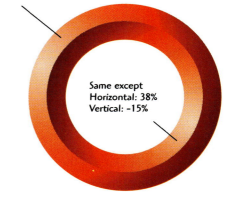

Same except
Horizontal: 38%
Vertical: –15%

3 What about diagonal segments? The vertical and horizontal segments in the octagon are shaded the same as their counterparts in the square. The diagonal segments are shaded as indicated, again consistent with the light source.

4 Circular objects are easily shaded with radial fountain fills. More complexly curved shapes require a different solution, which is discussed in steps 4 and 5 in the next section on Applying Shading Principles to the Letters.

Besides affecting whether the object appears to protrude or retract, shading can also have an impact on an object's surface properties. In general, subtle differences between the light and dark sides would portray a surface with a dull or matte finish. Fountain fills give the illusion of a shiny surface. In general, the greater the difference in the color values for the fountain fills, the more reflective the surface appears. Just remember to keep the relative dark and light relationship consistent with the light source.

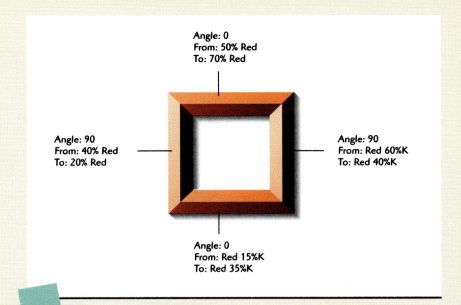

Angle: 0
From: 50% Red
To: 70% Red

Angle: 90
From: 40% Red
To: 20% Red

Angle: 90
From: Red 60%K
To: Red 40%K

Angle: 0
From: Red 15%K
To: Red 35%K

5 To create the appearance of a shinier surface, replace the single color fills with fountain fills. The angle and color values for Two Color Linear Fountain Fills given here are one example. For a final touch, add a shadow. (See Project 15.)

Applying Shading Principles to the Letters

1 Simple letter forms can be easily shaded by applying the principles learned in the preceding section on shading. In the case of this Gill Sans Italic *L*, ignore the slight slant and just apply the colors for straight verticals.

2 This Gill Sans *C* is also straightforward. Just apply the radial fountain fills used for the "donut" in step 4 in the preceding section, then shade the two vertical straight sections.

3 The curved sections of this Gill Sans *R* were shaded with radial fountain fills like the *C* in the previous step.

4 Unfortunately, some letter forms get a bit complicated, like this Times New Roman PS uppercase *S*. Radial fountain fills won't work on these serpentine sections. Two techniques that do work are blended ellipses and blended triangles. Just make sure the blend "from" color is the same as the solid fill of the object you're working on. Scale and align these blends over the letter section to be filled. Make sure that Automatically center new powerclip contents is turned off. Select all the blends. PowerClip into the letter segment.

5 For the side of the letter form farthest from the light source, remember to start with a darker shade solid fill. Most of the blends on this side go to a darker shade, in keeping with the orientation of the light source. Just remember to be consistent.

 HINT

Sometimes using either radial fountain fills, or the more complex PowerClip solution used for the S in steps 4 and 5, will work. In the case of the R in step 3, the fountain fills are much quicker and give the desired result.

6 Fill the flat sections as before, and you're done.

7 Just to show you that it can be done, here's the g. Radial fountain fills were used for the elliptical sections at the counter. Triangular blends were placed inside the rest of the sections to achieve the complex shading.

14

Using the Unique Lens Feature

What you will learn

- Casting a shadow that interacts with its background

- Using layers for efficient drawing management

ntroduced in version 5, and enhanced for version 6, Corel-DRAW's Lens feature represents an exciting step into interactive drawing. The Lens Roll-Up presents the user with 11 ways an object can interact with its background. Whether you move the object or alter the background, the lens interaction changes appropriately. In this exercise, the lens effects are used to create shadows, highlights, and magnification. You will learn how to draw a magnifying glass that really works. Move the magnifying glass over a new background and it reacts just like its real-life counterpart.

IMPORTANT NOTE: For CorelDRAW versions 5 and 6 only.

These colors are used in this section.

⬛	Black
⬜	White
🟥	Red 100%M, 100%Y
🟧	20% Red 20%M, 20%Y
🟧	60% Red 60%M, 60%Y

 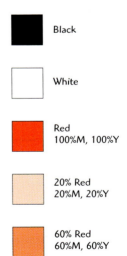

Drawing the Lens Holder

1 From the Layout menu, choose Layers Manager to bring up the Layers Roll-Up. Add the following layers in order: Lens Holder, Handle, Lens Glass, Shadow. Make Lens Holder the active and only visible layer by clicking on the icons. From the Layout menu, choose Grid and Ruler Setup, then set a grid with eight divisions per inch horizontal and vertical. Turn on Snap To Grid and Snap To Guidelines in the Layout menu. Move the ruler zero point near the top center of the page by dragging from the ruler intersection. Pull in guidelines, as indicated.

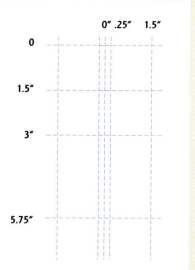

WARNING
The lens operations push your hardware. Screen redraw and print times go up, particularly if you stack several lens objects, as is done here.

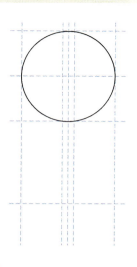

2 Snap a circle to the guidelines, as shown.

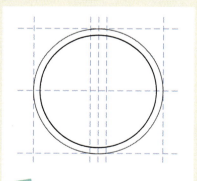

3 In the Scale & Mirror page of the Transform Roll-Up (Alt+F9), scale uniformly to 90%. Apply To Duplicate. In the Layers Roll-Up, Copy the duplicate to the Lens Glass layer.

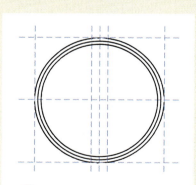

4 Blend the two circles in one step. Separate. Click away to deselect. Select the middle circle, and Ungroup. Copy the middle circle to the Shadow layer.

5 Duplicate the small circle (Plus [+] key on the numeric keypad). Shift+select the middle circle. Combine. Fill with a Radial Fountain Fill: From: Black; To: White; Horizontal: 35%; Vertical: -35%; Edge pad: 25%. Click OK. Click the X on the color palette with the right mouse button to turn off outline. Send To Back (Shift+PgDn).

Drawing the Handle

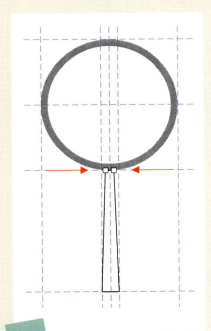

6 Select the small circle. Shift+select the big circle. Combine. Fill with a Radial Fountain Fill: From: Black; To: White; Horizontal: –35%; Vertical: 35%; Edge pad: 25%. Click OK. Turn off outline. Send To Back.

1 In the Layers Roll-Up, make the Handle layer the only visible layer. On the Handle layer, draw the rectangle shown. Convert To Curves. (Lens holder shown in gray for reference only.)

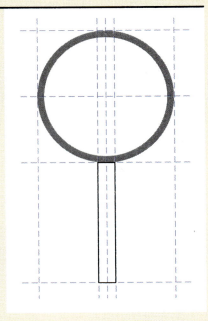

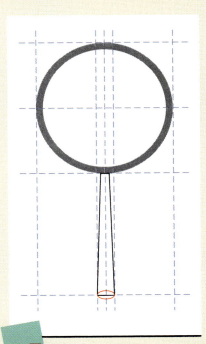

2 With the Shape Tool, select the top two nodes of the rectangle. In the Node Edit Roll-Up, click the Stretch and Scale Nodes button, then Shift+drag inward to about 50%. Turn off Snap To Guidelines if you're having trouble dragging the nodes off the guides.

3 Draw the ellipse shown (.25 inches high). The grid will maintain alignment.

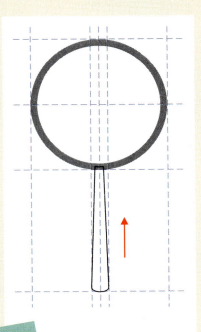

4 Select the ellipse and the trapezoid. Weld. Move straight up slightly using Nudge, so that the top of the handle will be hidden by the lens holder. Copy to the Shadow layer using the Layers Roll-Up.

5 Fill to 60% Red; no outline. Scale horizontally to 75%. Apply To Duplicate. Fill to Red.

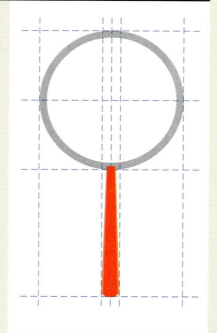

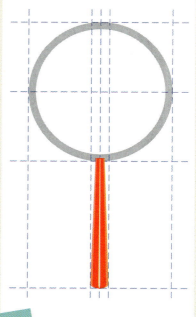

6 Scale horizontally to 20%. Apply To Duplicate. Fill to 20% Red.

7 Create a compound blend by first blending the two objects from step 5. Click off the blend to deselect. Zoom in and select the innermost object of the blend, then Shift+select the object from step 6. Blend.

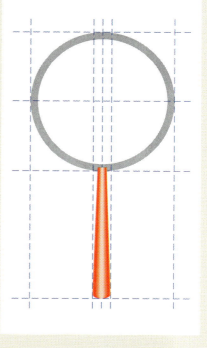

8 In the Layers Roll-Up, make all the named layers visible. Marquee-select the handle. Click a second time to display the rotate and skew handles. Move the center of rotation to the highlighted guideline intersection. Drag a rotation handle counterclockwise approximately 20 degrees.

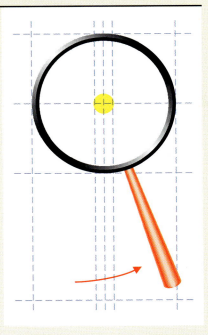

Drawing the Shadow

1 In the Layers Roll-Up, make the Shadow layer the only visible layer. Select the circle. Duplicate (Plus [+] key). Shift+select the handle. Move .3 inches horizontally, and –.3 inches vertically. (Magnifying glass shown in gray for reference only.)

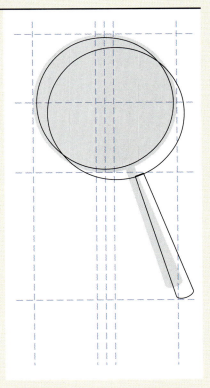

HINT

You can use the Color Limit Lens (under Lens in the Effects menu) filled with black to create a simple hard-edged shadow that will interact appropriately as you move it over different background objects. The Rate value determines the darkness of the shadow.

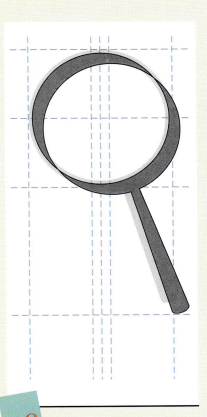

2 With the lower-right circle and the handle selected, Weld. Shift+select the other circle. Combine. Assign no outline. In the Lens Roll-Up, choose Color Limit; set Color: Black; Rate: 40. Apply.

Adding the Lens Effects

HINT

As an alternative, you may want to experiment with CorelDRAW 6's Fisheye lens. This will both magnify and distort the underlying image.

1 In the Layers Roll-Up, make the Lens Glass layer visible, and all the other layers invisible. Select the circle. Assign no outline. In the Lens Roll-Up, choose the Color Limit Lens; set Color: Black; Rate: 10%. Apply. This will have the effect of darkening the objects seen through the glass a very slight amount. (The colored lines in the background are shown as reference to the different lens effects used in this section.)

2 With the circle selected, Duplicate. In the Lens Roll-Up, select the Magnify lens. Enter the desired magnification value (2x here). Apply. The stacked lenses will add to the effects, so the area under the lens is both darkened slightly and magnified.

Draw the highlight. In the Lens Roll-Up, assign the Brighten lens. Choose an appropriate Rate (50% here).

4 Turn on all the named layers. Adjust the shadow as desired.

HINT

The farther the shadow is moved away, the higher the apparent position of the magnifying glass.

15

Casting Shadows

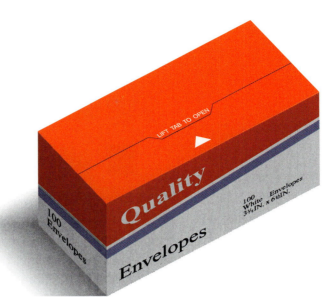

What you will learn

- Understanding what makes a shadow hard edged, soft edged, or fading

- Mastering techniques for creating hard, soft, and fading shadows

- Casting a shadow over a multicolored background

Realistic cast shadows are essential to a three-dimensional illustration. Shadows provide information about the shape of an object and its location relative to other objects. Shadows touching the base of an object anchor it to the background. Drop shadows suspend an object above the background. Shadows can be soft or hard edged, and may fade as they recede from the base of the object.

This project shows how to cast shadows from a single primary light source and the resulting ambient light. Shadows cast from multiple light sources are not only more difficult to render, but also tend to be confusing to interpret. A single light source provides the best information for the clearest interpretation by the viewer.

Before proceeding with the examples, the structure of a shadow will be discussed. Hard-edged shadows are considered typical of natural light, and soft shadows typical of artificial light. In truth, the extent to which a shadow is soft edged is dependent on the geometry between the light source, subject, and background, and not on its origin.

These colors are used in this section.

	White		
	20%K		Green 50%C, 50%Y
	30%K		Green 40%K 50%C, 50%Y, 40%K
	40%K		Deep Yellow 20%M, 100%Y
	50%K		Deep Yellow 50%K 20%M, 100%Y, 50%K

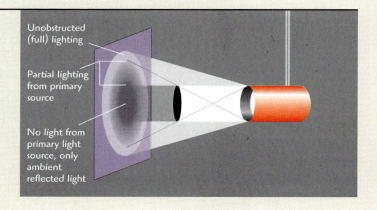

Unobstructed (full) lighting

Partial lighting from primary source

No light from primary light source, only ambient reflected light

1 In this figure, a light illumi-nates a circular disk, which casts a shadow on a vertical background. The beam is not focused, so light from the top of the lamp, for example, illuminates the bottom of the disk as well as the top. This is what creates the soft shadow. In the darkest part of the shadow, the disk blocks all direct light from reaching the background. In the area outside the shadow, the disk doesn't prevent any light from reaching the background.

In between, the disk prevents some of the light from reaching the back-ground.

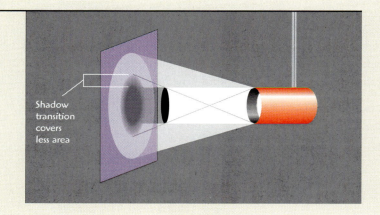

Shadow transition covers less area

2 Everything else being equal, as the disk is moved closer to the vertical back-ground, the shadow transition area becomes smaller.

3 Similarly, as the light source is made smaller and/or located farther away, the transition area also is reduced. For a pinpoint light source, or one located an infinite distance away, there would be no transition area and a hard shadow would be the result.

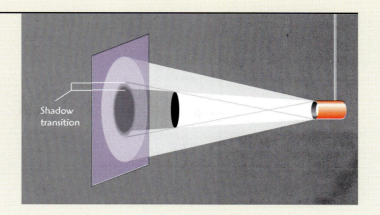

Shadow transition

4 Light reflected from surrounding objects creates an ambient light that can cause a shadow to fade as it gets farther away from the base of the object. Note that this fading effect is different from the soft-edged shadows discussed above.

Casting Generic Shadows

This example shows how to cast a generic shadow using a common technique in computer illustration. When the shadow is made to fade completely to the background color, this method can be used to represent a soft shadow cast from artificial light. It's easy and usually conveys the desired effect; but rather than being a true soft shadow, it's a hard-edged shadow that fades completely to the background color. The severe fade is used to represent a soft edge. The generic shadow can also be constructed so that the fade is not so severe. Remember the example showing that the farther the object casting the shadow is from the background, the softer the shadow. Short objects with artificial lighting can be realistically rendered with hard-edged shadows, assuming the light source isn't too near or from an extremely low angle.

Finally, since sunlight casts a harder edged shadow, this method can also be used to cast shadows from natural light.

1 a) Draw a shape to outline the base of the object casting the shadow. Fill to 40%K.
b) Click on the shape and drag in the direction of the shadow, pressing the right mouse button to leave the original. Under Order, choose Back One. For a shadow that fades completely, fill with White. For a harder shadow, fill with some percentage of black (less than 40%). The more black, the harder the shadow.

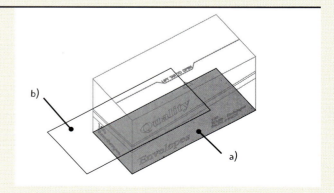

b)

a)

2 Select both objects. Blend. Move the blend To Back. Here's the result when the blend from color is white, frequently used to represent a soft shadow cast from artificial light.

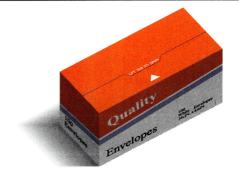

3 Here the blend from color is 20%K, giving the appearance of a hard-edged shadow.

4 The real fun starts when you cast a shadow over a multicolored background. Here the shadow crosses a green rectangle. First, make sure Automatically center new powerclip contents is turned off.

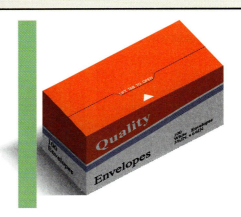

5 Select the shadow blend. Press the Plus [+] key on the numeric keypad to Duplicate the blend without moving it. Zoom in and select the left blend object. Change its fill to Green. Select the right blend object. Change its fill to Green 40%K. CorelDRAW will automatically reblend with the new fill colors. Preview the image and you'll see the original blend display, and then the green blend appear on top.

6 Select the green blend. PowerClip into the green rectangle. If necessary, move the rectangle To Front.

Creating Soft Shadows Using Blended Lines

Soft shadows cast from natural light occur under a variety of circumstances that require different solutions. In this next example, soft drop shadows of complex shapes are easily rendered by blending two copies of the original object, one outlined with a wide line and the other with a thin one.

1 Duplicate the original object. In the Outline Pen dialog, stroke with a relatively wide line width (5 points or so for this size object). Check the round Corners option. If you'll be scaling the object later, check Scale with image. Assign White for both the line and fill color. (Black was used for the line color in steps 1 and 2, just so you could see it.)

3 Marquee-select and Blend. Place the original object on top.

2 Duplicate (Plus [+] key on the numeric keypad). Change the fill and line colors to 30%K. Assign a hairline width.

Rendering Soft-fading Shadows Using Blended Fountain Fills

Here's another situation where you have a soft shadow cast by an artificial light. In this case, however, ambient light reflected off the walls in the room will tend to cause the shadow to fade rather severely. One approach is to blend between two linear fountain fills, accomplishing both the soft edge and fade.

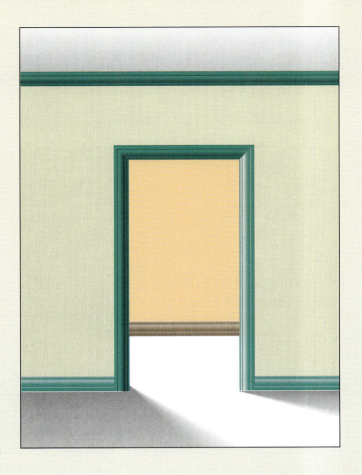

HINT

Blended fountain fills take a long time to print and redraw on the screen. You'll experience the least frustration if you stick to angles in 90-degree multiples.

1 Draw the initial shadow shape. Fill with White.

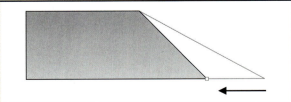

2 Duplicate. With the Shape Tool, drag the indicated node straight left. Fill with a Linear Fountain Fill: From: 20%K; To: 40%K; Angle: 90. Blend the two.

Rendering Hard-edged Shadows

While it's true that the sun is neither a pinpoint light source nor an infinite distance away, relative to most other common light sources, it is close enough to these requirements so that shadows cast from sunlight are characteristically rendered as hard edged. (With a low sun and a tall object, you'll notice a slight softness to the shadow.) Sunlit shadows are also typically rendered as fading shadows. Realistically, the amount of fade can be minimal, but is frequently exaggerated for stylistic considerations.

1 Starting from the object whose shadow you want to cast, select the shapes that define its contour. Duplicate. Weld.

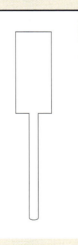

2 With the shadow contour selected, drag the top-middle handle straight down to scale vertically.

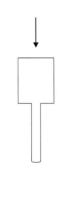

3 Click again to bring up the skew and rotate handles. Drag the top-middle handle straight left to skew the shadow. Fill with a Linear Fountain Fill. You can blend all the way to the background color for a complete fade, or add some black for a partial fade, just like the blends used in the generic shadow. The following values were used here: Angle: 90; From: 50%K; To: White. Place the shadow behind the original object.

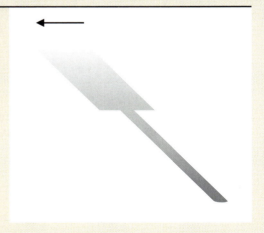

Enhancing with the Power of a Shadow

This fun exercise demonstrates how much visual information a simple shadow can convey. Even with a difficult-to-read font filled to the same color as the background, the word *shadow* is easily read.

1 Over your background (Deep Yellow here), type the word *shadow*. Fill to the background color. (Black outline shown here for clarity only.)

2 Select Copy from the Edit menu. Reselect the original. Drag down and to the right. Click the right mouse button to leave a copy. Send Back One. Reselect the top-left copy of the word. Change its fill color by adding approximately 50% Black. (Deep Yellow 50%K was used here.)

3 Blend. Note how easily the generic shadow method casts a shadow for this intricate shape.

4 Paste. Fill to White. Nudge up and to the left. In the final version, this process will result in a line highlight, so only move it a small distance.

5 Paste. The simple line highlight and generic shadow have effectively raised the word from the background.

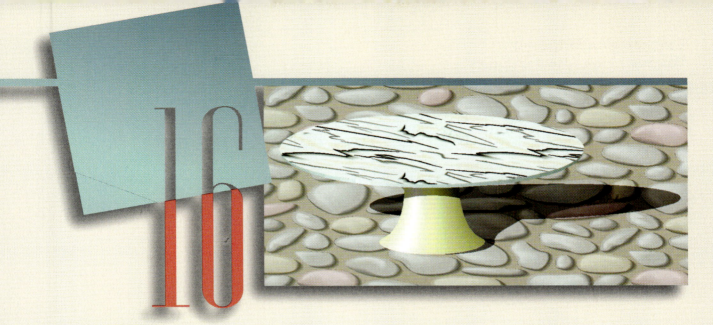

16

Making a Seamless Pattern

What you will learn

- Creating a seamless pattern
- Mastering irregular shading and highlights typical of objects in nature

The Pattern Fills feature is generally used to fill an object with an obviously repeating pattern, like a brick wall. But what if you want a pattern that does not appear to repeat, such as a cloudy sky, a marble tabletop, or a stone floor? There's a trick to it, which you'll learn in this project.

These colors are used in this section.

	Gray Stone 5%C, 20%K	Red Stone 3%M, 3%Y, 20%K	Yellow Stone 5%Y, 20%K
Cement 5%Y, 25%K	Gray Stone Shadow 5%C, 50%K	Red Stone Shadow 3%M, 3%Y, 50%K	Yellow Stone Shadow 5%Y, 50%K (same as Cement Shadow)
Cement Shadow 5%Y, 50%K	Gray Stone Highlight 5%C, 10%K	Red Stone Highlight 3%M, 3%Y, 10%K	Yellow Stone Highlight 5%Y, 10%K

Creating the Illusion of Patterns That Don't Repeat

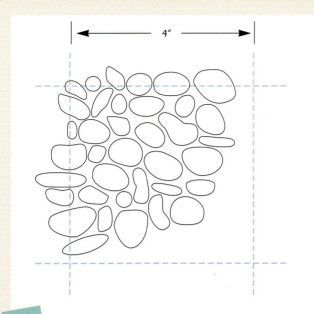

1 In Options under Tools, set Undo levels to at least 2. Create the following layers: Stone, Shadow, Cement. Place two vertical and two horizontal guidelines to form a 4-inch square. On the Stone layer, draw some basic stone shapes that overlap the top and left guidelines. Draw more shapes inside the square, leaving the right and bottom edges untouched.

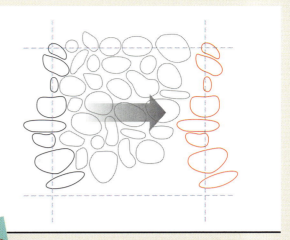

2 When the square is fairly well filled out, select the objects overlapping the left guide. Then, in the Position page of the Transform Roll-Up, enter Horizontal 4 inches and Vertical 0 inches. Apply To Duplicate.

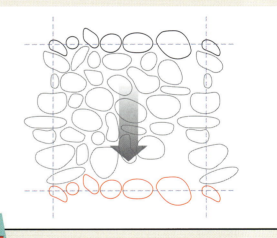

3 Repeat for the objects overlapping the top guide, only enter Horizontal 0 inches and Vertical –4 inches. If you've placed any stones too close to the edges in the previous steps, there may be overlapping objects. If any exist, Undo twice, make corrections, and try again. The basic concept for creating seamless tiles is to place exact duplicates on opposite sides of your guidelines.

Since you'll also want to add shadows and shading on the stones first, once you're satisfied with the placement, Undo twice so the image looks like that in step 1.

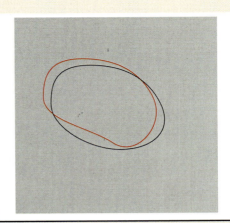

4 Make the Cement layer the active layer. With Snap To Guidelines on, snap a 4-inch square to the guidelines. Fill with the Cement color, then lock the Cement layer. Marquee-select all the stone outlines. In the Layers Roll-Up, Copy To the Shadow layer. Make the Shadow layer invisible.

5 The next few steps show how to add shading to, and create a shadow for, a stone. You'll have to repeat these steps for each stone. Select a stone outline. Use the Position page of the Transform Roll-Up to move approximately -.050 inches Horizontal and .050 inches Vertical. Apply To Duplicate. Select the new object. Using the Shape Tool, move nodes and control points to add some variation so that the shading will show irregularities typical of a stone smoothed by years of erosion.

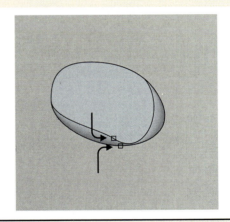

6 Select the new, reshaped object. In the Intersect Roll-Up, check Leave Original Target Object, then click on Intersect With. Click on the original stone shape. Fill the top object with the Gray Stone color. Select the bottom object. Fill with Gray Stone Shadow.

7 Select the two objects, and Blend. It's likely you won't get the desired results because the intersect operation added nodes to the newly created shape. If so, Undo. Equalize the number of nodes in the two objects by adding nodes to one or deleting from the other. (Either use the Node Edit Roll-Up or select the object with the Shape Tool and use the Plus [+] and Minus [-] keys on the numeric keypad.) Then, in the Blend Roll-Up, click the compass icon, then the Map Nodes button. Then, click on an adjacent node from each object. Click Apply.

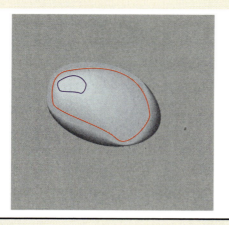

8 Draw an outline filling most of the unshaded portion of the stone. Fill with the Gray Stone color (red outline for clarity only). Duplicate, stretch down, and reshape as desired (blue outline for clarity). Since you'll be using these shapes to create a soft highlight on the stone, once again you'll want to show some irregularities in the outlines. Fill with Gray Stone Highlight. Select both objects. Blend.

9 Make the Stone layer invisible and the Shadow layer visible. Fill the stone shape with the Cement Shadow color. Use the Position page of the Transform Roll-Up to move Horizontal .050 inches Horizontal and Vertical -.050 inches. Apply To Duplicate. Fill with the Cement color. Send To Back. Select both. Blend.

HINT

If you want to mix your own stone colors, stick with fairly muted tones which won't be so obvious as a repeating tile in the pattern fill.

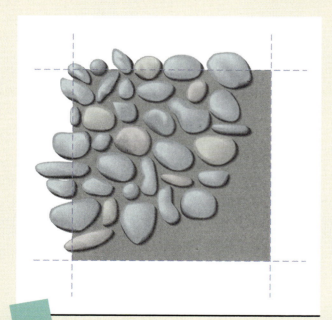

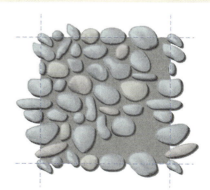

10 Repeat steps 5 through 9 for all the stones. For variation, try using the Red and Yellow Stone colors.

11 With all the named layers visible, use the Position page of the Transform Roll-Up to copy all the objects that overlap the left guideline 4 inches to the right, and all objects that overlap the top guideline 4 inches down, as in steps 2 and 3.

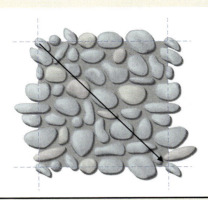

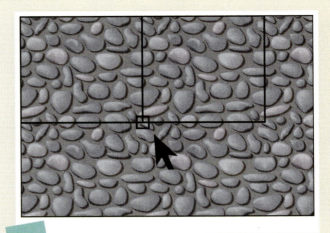

12 Fill in the spaces by adding new stones, including all shading, highlights, and shadows. Be careful not to overlap any guidelines. You're now ready to create the pattern fill. First make sure all layers are unlocked. Turn on Snap To Guidelines. Select Tools ➢ Create ➢ Pattern. For type, click Full Color, then OK. Drag the crosshairs from the top-left guideline intersection to the bottom-right intersection. When the prompt "Create pattern with selected area?" appears, click OK. Type in a name for the pattern. Click Save. Watch the hourglass spin around for a while. When it's done, your new pattern should appear in Corel's Vector Pattern palette.

13 To fill an object with the new pattern, access the Fill Roll-Up, and click the Vector Pattern button (double-headed arrow). Click in the preview box to access the Vector Pattern palette. Scroll down, find the new pattern, and double-click it. After a few moments it will appear in the preview box. Click Tile. Two rectangles and a node will appear in your object. Make the tile size fairly large by dragging the node. For a pattern like this, making the tile too small can make the repeating objects noticeable. Click Apply.

VARIATIONS

It doesn't take a very complex pattern to make something that looks fairly random. This pattern was created from basic lines and circles using the technique described in steps 1 through 13.

Adobe Photoshop owners have access to excellent random and repetitive seamless patterns located in the Photoshop\Patterns directory. Simply import the pattern using CorelDRAW's Adobe Illustrator import filter. Ungroup the imported image, fill as you like, and create a pattern from it. Instead of using guidelines, turn on Snap To Objects and use the box that imports with the Adobe Photoshop pattern as a guide to create the pattern fill.

Making a Repetitive Seamless Pattern

Creating repetitive seamless patterns is much easier than creating a pattern that looks random. The only trick is making the pattern seamless. The same principle of making the right/left and top/bottom sides match applies as used in the stone floor example.

1 Draw a 2-inch square. Position text or clipart over the top-left corner. Draw crossmarks, shown in red above, over the intersection of the top-left corner.

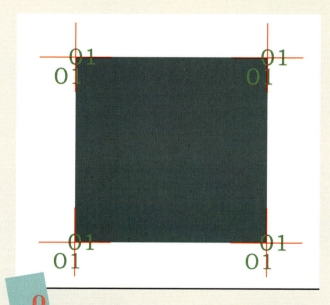

2 Duplicate the text or clipart and the crossmarks. Use the crossmarks to align the duplicates to the remaining corners.

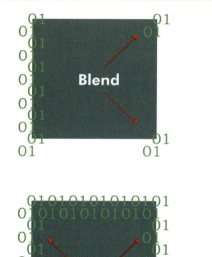

3 Delete the crossmarks. Blend between each corner from top to bottom. Separate and Ungroup the blends. Then, Blend between left and right corresponding elements. It may take a little experimentation to determine how many Blend steps it will take to fill up the square.

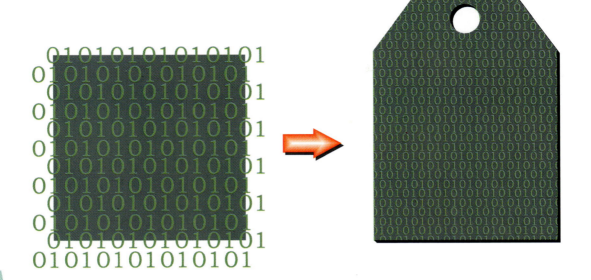

4 When the square is filled
with blended elements,
create a pattern using
the square, with Snap To Objects
on as a guide.

Grids and grids made from
Guidelines can be used to create
patterns as well. In this example, a
quarter–inch grid was created with
Guidelines. Then, shapes and control
points were snapped to various
intersections with the Snap To
Guidelines option on. An endless
variety of patterns can be created by
this method.

Repeated shapes and elements
are also an easy source for pattern
fills. This pattern utilizes offsetting
rectangles with repeated holes and
twine to create a pattern that
resembles pleated blinds.

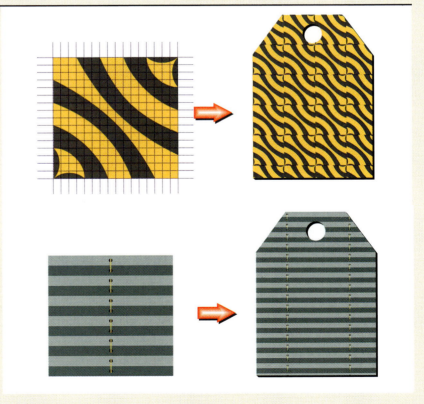

This pattern fill was created with the "corrugated metal" technique discussed in Project 5, using straight-line segments instead of curved-line segments. The extrusion was the same distance as the length of the line segments to create a square.

Finally, clipart can be an excellent source for repetitive patterns. This piece of clipart from Image Club was filled with custom colors to create a rich tile pattern fill.

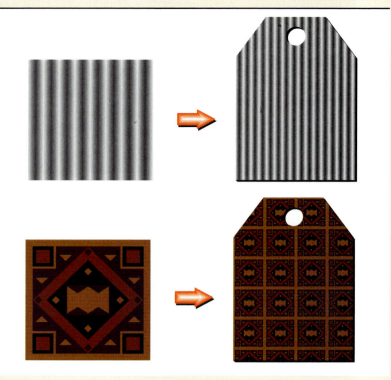

HINT

If you rotate an object that's filled with a pattern (or skew, add perspective, or envelope edit for that matter), the object will be transformed, but the fill will remain the same.

A workaround is to first export the image in Encapsulated PostScript format (EPS, Placeable). Don't bother including an image header. Then, import the image back in using the PostScript Interpreted format. This process will convert the pattern to its individual components. (Look at your reimported image in Wireframe mode to see this clearly.) If your pattern is very complex, there may be quite a few objects, so screen redraw and print times could suffer. Also, file sizes can get huge in a hurry. However, these individual shapes will transform properly.

One last word of caution. The Postscript Interpreted filter is not infallible. Occasionally you will notice slight discrepancies between the original pattern and the reimported version.

17

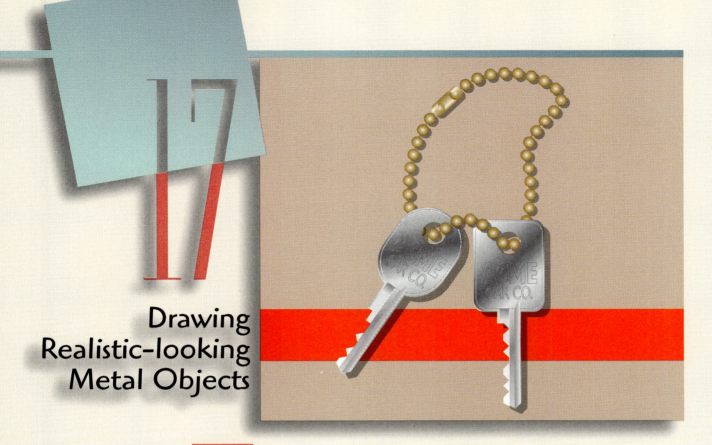

Drawing Realistic-looking Metal Objects

What you will learn

- Rendering metals

- Drawing finely stamped details

- Using advanced Blend features

- Interweaving objects with a nested PowerClip technique

- Constructing images efficiently

T his key and chain exercise may look simple at first, but it provides a few interesting challenges. The advanced Blend and PowerClip features will be put through their paces to create a chain and interweave it with the keys. Techniques for rendering different types of metals, and drawing finely impressed details like the stamped letters on the faces of the keys, will also be presented.

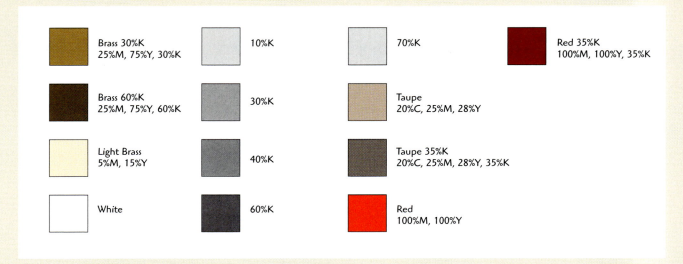

Brass 30%K
25%M, 75%Y, 30%K

10%K

70%K

Red 35%K
100%M, 100%Y, 35%K

Brass 60%K
25%M, 75%Y, 60%K

30%K

Taupe
20%C, 25%M, 28%Y

Light Brass
5%M, 15%Y

40%K

Taupe 35%K
20%C, 25%M, 28%Y, 35%K

White

60%K

Red
100%M, 100%Y

These colors are used in this section.

Drawing the Keys

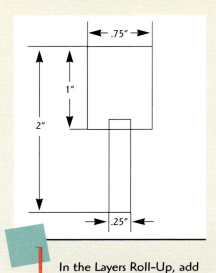

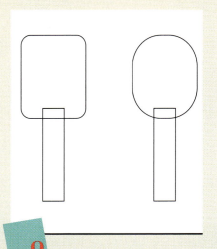

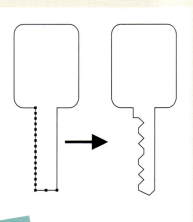

1 In the Layers Roll-Up, add the following layers in order: Key, Chain, Shadow. Set Grid Frequency to 16 per inch. Turn on Snap To Grid. Turn off Automatically center new powerclip contents. On the Key layer, draw and overlap two rectangles. Select both. Drag straight right, and click the right mouse button to create a duplicate.

2 With the Shape Tool, round the corners of the top rectangles, as shown. This creates the basic shapes of one rectangular key and one oval key.

3 Select the two objects from one key. Weld. Add a bunch of nodes as shown, using the Node Edit Roll-Up or the Plus (+) key on the numeric keypad. Then, rearrange to create the teeth. The grid should maintain alignment.

4 Repeat for the other key.

5 Draw and position the .25-inch-diameter circles, as shown. Select a circle and key. Combine, creating a key with a hole in it. Repeat for the other key. Select both keys. In the Layers Roll-Up, Copy To the Shadow layer. Back on the Key layer, fill each key with a Custom Linear Fountain Fill, adding several alternating bands of different shades of gray (no outline). The exact parameters used are up to your artistic eye. The following is used in the example: Angle: -45; Position 0%: White; Position 4%: White; Position 19%: 30%K; Position 31%: 60%K; Position 47%: 10%K; Position 65%: 40%K; Position 100%: White.

From: 10% Black
To: 40% Black
Angle: 90 deg.

From: White
To: 10% Black
Angle: 90 deg.

From: 40% Black
To: 10% Black
Angle: 0 deg.

6 Turn off Snap To Grid. Draw two rectangles and one modified rectangle. (For the right object, draw a rectangle, Convert To Curves, move the top-left node straight down.) Fill with Two Color Linear Fountain Fills, as shown. Put a Taupe-colored background on the Shadow layer.

7 Turn on Snap To Objects for this step only. Using the Freehand or Beziér Tool, add the two line highlights, using white hairlines (shown as black for clarity).

8 Select the three rectangular objects and the lines. PowerClip into the key.

9 Repeat for the other key.

10 To add finely stamped details typically found on keys, create the detail and assign a hairline white outline, no fill. Duplicate (Plus [+] key on numeric keypad). Nudge the duplicate up and to the left just a little. Change the line color to black or a dark shade of gray.

11 Make sure the Key and Key Shadow layer are both visible. Marquee-select one key (so that both a key and its hidden shadow are selected). Rotate and move the key into position.

HINT
When you rotate objects filled with linear fountain fills in CorelDRAW, the fill is spread out over the objects highlighting box. The result is that objects that previously showed the entire range of specified colors now show only a portion of the colors. To correct this, go back into the Fountain Fill dialog and increase the Edge-pad value. You may want to do this for the rectangular objects PowerClipped into the rotated key.

12 Make the Key layer temporarily invisible. On the Shadow layer, select the shadows. Move down and to the right about .06 inches. For a solid background, fill to the background color plus about 35%K added (Taupe 35%K). (Key outlines shown for reference only.)

13 For multicolored backgrounds, duplicate the shadows. Fill the duplicates to the second background color plus 35%K. (Here the new background color is Red, and the new shadow color is Red 35%K.) Select the new shadows. PowerClip into the red rectangle. If necessary, move the rectangle in front of the original shadow.

Drawing the Clasp

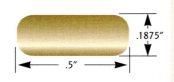

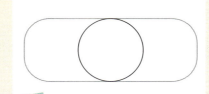

1 Turn on Snap To Grid. On the Chain layer (Key and Shadow layers invisible for now), draw a .5-inch-wide by .1875-inch-high rectangle. With the Shape Tool, round the corners. Fill with a Custom Linear Fountain Fill: Position 0%: Brass 30%K; Position 25%: Light Brass; Position 100%: Brass 30%K; Angle: 90.

2 Working in Wireframe, draw a .1875-inch circle. Align to the center of the rounded rectangle. Convert To Curves.

3 With the Shape Tool, Ctrl+drag the side nodes of the circle straight out to the sides of the rounded rectangle.

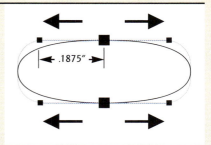

4 Drag the control points from the top and bottom nodes out horizontally .1875 inches, as shown.

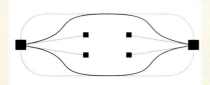

5 In the Node Edit Roll-Up, convert the left and right nodes to Cusp Nodes. Drag the control points, as shown. The grid will snap them to the exact locations indicated.

6 Back in Preview mode, select the original rounded rectangle. Duplicate (Plus [+] key). Shift+select the object from the previous step. Combine. Assign the same fountain fill as in step 1, only set the custom color position to 75%.

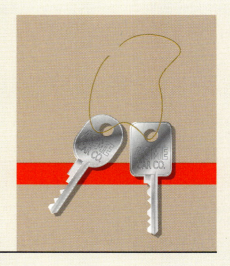

Drawing the Chain

1 Temporarily make the Key and Shadow layers visible. On the Chain layer, draw a curved line overlapping the two keyholes, draping it so that it has the natural shape of a key chain. Assign a 1-point line width, and the Brass 30%K color.

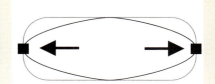

3 Rotate and move the clasp into its approximate position. At this point, the clasp looks a little large, so stretch it down for a better fit. With the Shape Tool, adjust the endpoints of the line for a perfect fit, so that the end chain links just fit inside the clasp. (The Status Line should say Control Curve on Chain. Then make the adjustments.)

2 Make the Key and Shadow layers invisible. On the Chain layer, draw a .125-inch-diameter circle. Fill with a Custom Radial Fountain Fill; Position 0%: Brass 60%K; Position 25%: Brass 30%K; Position 100%: Light Brass; Edge pad: 10%. Duplicate. Select both circles, and open the Blend Roll-Up. Select the path icon. Click New Path. Then, click on the line from the previous step. Click Full Path. Enter an estimate for the number of steps. Click Apply. Based on the result, enter a revised estimate for the number of steps, and click Apply again. Repeat until the links have the correct spacing.

4 Select the top section of the clasp. Send To Front. At this point you'll notice the same problem with the rotated linear fountain fills as before, so go into the Fountain Fill dialog and increase the Edge-pad values to 35% or so. The best value for your clasp may be different depending on how much it's rotated. If necessary, select the path (control curve) from the blend group, and send To Back.

5 Now that the chain is in its final position, use the Layers Roll-Up to put a copy on the Shadow layer. Make the Shadow layer the only visible layer. Move the clasp and links right and down approximately .03 inches. Separate the blended links. Delete the line and the top of the clasp. Fill with the background color plus 35% black (Taupe 35%K). Ungroup the links. Your shadow layer should look something like this.

Putting It All Together

1 Make all the layers visible.
Draw a rectangle overlap-
ping the two keyholes, as
shown. (Black outline for clarity
only.) Separate and Ungroup the
blend on the chain layer. Marquee-
select the links, and link shadows
shown. Shift+select the rectangle to
delete it from the selection. Zoom in
and Shift+select the line (originally
the control curve for the blend) to
add it to the selection. Duplicate
(Plus [+] key). PowerClip into the
rectangle.

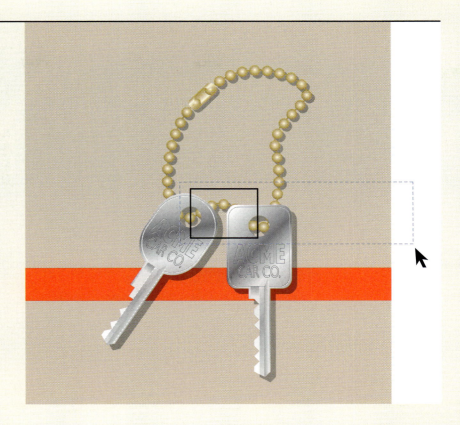

2 With the rectangle selected, choose Effects ➤
PowerClip ➤ Edit
Contents. Select the circles for the
chain-link shadow. Change them to
a color appropriate for a shadow cast
over the keys—for example, 70%K.
Then, choose Effects ➤ PowerClip
➤ Finish Editing This Level.

3 Duplicate the PowerClip rectangle from the previous step (Plus [+]
key). PowerClip into one of the keys. PowerClip the original rectangle into the remaining key.

Tips and Tricks for Rendering Transparency

What you will learn

- Using glares, tonal changes, edge definition, and refraction to render transparent objects

- Mastering efficient object-construction techniques

How do you draw something you can see through? By drawing the objects behind as they are altered by the transparent object. It is this ambiguous nature of transparency that makes it such a fascinating and tricky subject.

Examine the windshield from outside your car. Under most lighting conditions, the interior of the car is clearly defined where the windshield appears dark, but where highlights or reflections are visible, the interior is obscured. This is an important technique to use in creating transparent effects—either the reflection of some specific element in the environment or the reflection of some nonspecific

light source in the form of a highlight.

From inside the car now, roll down the side window part way. The top edge of the window is readily defined. Most edges of transparent objects are either opaque or they radically distort the objects behind, providing a distinct edge definition. You may also notice that objects behind the window are darker than objects seen through the open portion. Sure, your car probably has tinted glass, but this is also true for untinted transparent objects. In most cases, this is a subtle effect, but in the case of varnish or lacquer on wood, for example, the darkening effect and increase in contrast are quite remarkable.

Back in your house, partly fill a glass with water, then put a pencil, brush, or similar object in the water. Place the glass against an even-colored background, and observe.

Notice how the pencil appears to bend where it enters the surface of the water, disappear where it intersects the meniscus, and reappear in an offset position when viewed through the side surface of the water—a phenomenon known as refraction. Depending on your lighting, you may also note that the water and the thick bottom of the glass have a unique glowing effect. This is typical of thick transparent objects.

White	25% Blue 25%C, 5%M		
10%K	75% Blue 75%C, 15%M	Blue 35%K 100%C, 20%M, 35%K	Red 100%M, 100%Y
20%K	Blue 20%K 100%C, 20%M, 20%K	Blue 50%K 100%C, 20%M, 50%K	20% Red 20%M, 20%Y
15%Blue 15%C, 3%M	Blue 25%K 100%C, 20%M, 25%K	15% Blue 5%K 15%C, 3%M, 5%K	25% Red 25%M, 25%Y

These colors are used in this section.

Rendering the Glass

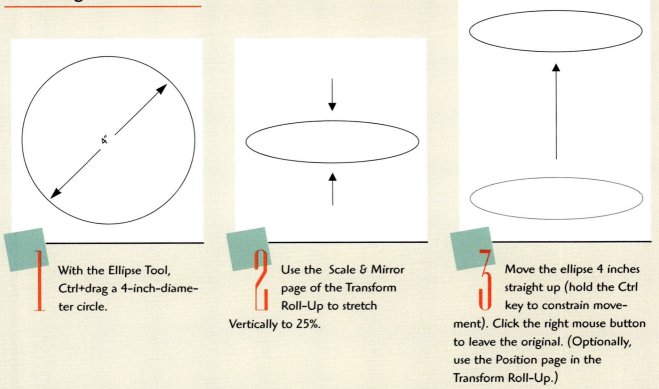

1 With the Ellipse Tool, Ctrl+drag a 4-inch-diameter circle.

2 Use the Scale & Mirror page of the Transform Roll-Up to stretch Vertically to 25%.

3 Move the ellipse 4 inches straight up (hold the Ctrl key to constrain movement). Click the right mouse button to leave the original. (Optionally, use the Position page in the Transform Roll-Up.)

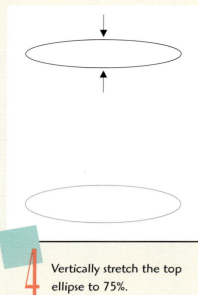

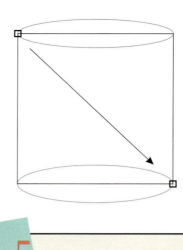

4 Vertically stretch the top ellipse to 75%.

5 Copy the two ellipses to the clipboard. With Snap To Objects on, draw a rectangle by dragging from the top-left point to the lower-right point.

6 Select the three objects. Weld. Fill with a Custom Linear Fountain Fill: Angle: 0; Position 0%: 10%K; Position 5%: Blue 25%K; Position 25%: White; Position 95%: Blue 25%K; Position 100%: 20%K.

HINT

Objects copied to the clipboard from Corel-DRAW will Paste back in their original positions. This is a handy way to temporarily store extra copies of objects, as long as you don't forget and accidentally copy something else to the clipboard.

7 Paste. If you haven't moved anything in the meantime, the two ellipses will be aligned as shown.

8 In the Scale & Mirror page of the Transform Roll-Up, uniformly Scale the top ellipse to 90%. Apply To Duplicate. Uniformly Scale the bottom ellipse to 90%. Apply.

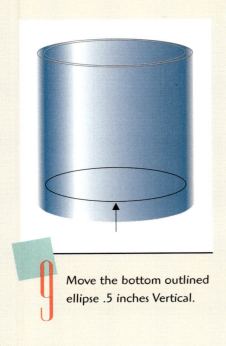

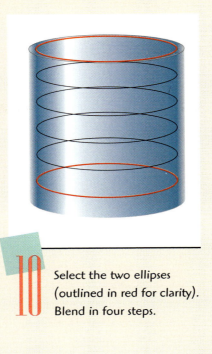

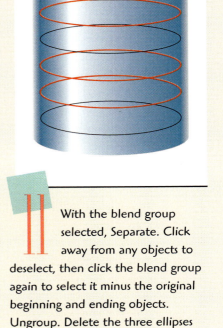

9 Move the bottom outlined ellipse .5 inches Vertical.

10 Select the two ellipses (outlined in red for clarity). Blend in four steps.

11 With the blend group selected, Separate. Click away from any objects to deselect, then click the blend group again to select it minus the original beginning and ending objects. Ungroup. Delete the three ellipses shown in red.

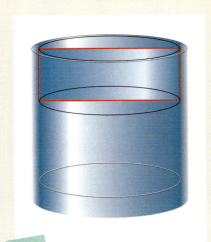

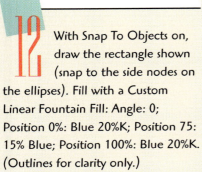

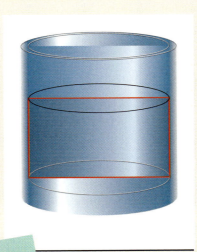

12 With Snap To Objects on, draw the rectangle shown (snap to the side nodes on the ellipses). Fill with a Custom Linear Fountain Fill: Angle: 0; Position 0%: Blue 20%K; Position 75: 15% Blue; Position 100%: Blue 20%K. (Outlines for clarity only.)

13 Draw another rectangle. Fill with a Custom Linear Fountain Fill: Angle: 0; Position 0%: Blue 35%K; Position 75%: 25% Blue; Position 100%: Blue 35%K. Move the four ellipses To Front.

14 Fill the larger top ellipse to 15% Blue 5%K.

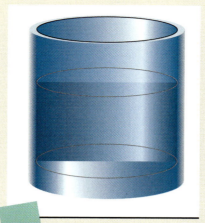

15 Fill the smaller top ellipse with a Custom Linear Fountain Fill: Angle: 0; Position 0%: Blue 20%K; Position 75%: White; Position 100%: Blue 20%K.

16 Fill the outlined ellipse with a Two Color Linear Fountain Fill: Angle: 85; From: Blue 50%K; To: White.

17 Uniformly scale the ellipse from the previous step to 97%. Apply To Duplicate. Fill with a Custom Linear Fountain Fill: Angle: 85; Position 0%: Blue 25%K; Position 50%: Blue 25%K; Position 100%: 25% Blue.

18 Fill the large ellipse at the bottom of the glass to Blue 25%K. Uniformly scale to 10%. Apply To Duplicate. Move up and to the right. Fill to 25% Blue. Select the two. Blend.

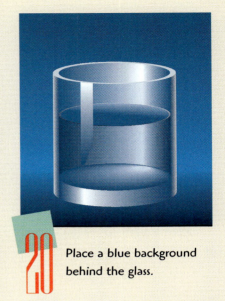

19 Draw a shape similar to the one shown. Fill with a Two Color Linear Fountain Fill: Angle: 90; From: Blue 25%K; To: White.

20 Place a blue background behind the glass.

Tricky Stuff: Putting the Brush in the Glass

1 If you're looking for more of a challenge, try placing a paintbrush inside the glass. Use the paintbrush from Project 12. Change the color of the handle to Red, and simplify the brush tip. Rotate and position the brush in the glass, as shown.

2 To make it easier to see progress in subsequent steps as the brush is placed inside the glass, select the brush handle blend and send To Back.

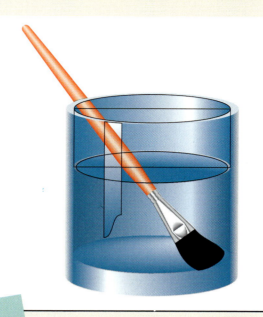

3 Select the brush handle blend. Duplicate (Plus [+] key). PowerClip into the outlined rectangle. The brush will display only up to the meniscus because the ellipses are in front of the rectangle.

4 Do the same thing for the objects from steps 12, 15, 17, and 19 in the preceding section.

5 The brush handle should cover only the back lip of the glass. Draw a small rectangle, as shown. The rectangle should have no outline and no fill, but is shown here outlined in black for clarity.

6 Duplicate the brush handle blend. PowerClip it into the rectangle.

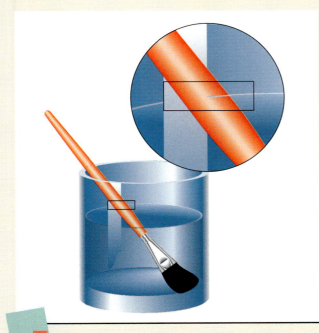

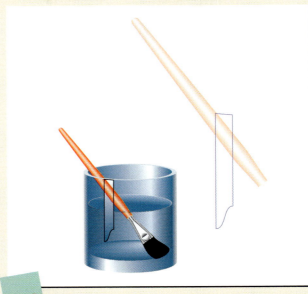

HINT

When editing the contents of a PowerClip container, DRAW will display only the contents in full color, and the container will be outlined in blue. No other objects in the image will be visible.

7 It's difficult to see, but there's a thin sliver of water showing at the meniscus where the brush should be (magnified view). Duplicate the brush handle blend. PowerClip it into the rectangle shown (outline for clarity only).

8 Select the glare, and move To Front. Choose Effects ➤ PowerClip ➤ Edit Contents. Lighten the brush handle under the glare by changing the "from" and "to" blend colors to 25% Red and White. Choose Effects ➤ PowerClip ➤ Finish Editing This Level.

9 Select the outlined rectangle and Edit Contents. Select the handle blend. Use the Position page of the Transform Roll-Up to move straight left, –.10 inches or so Horizontal. Whatever measure you use, remember the value. Finish Editing This Level. At this point the handle no longer lines up with the ferrule and bristles. Select them. Use the Transform Roll-Up to move the same distance as the brush handle.

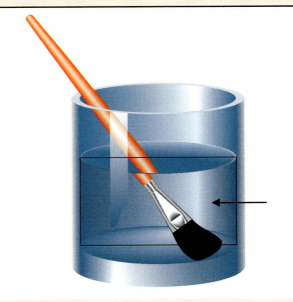

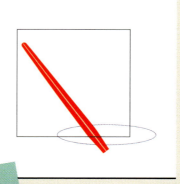

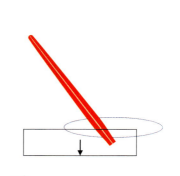

10 Select the outlined ellipse and Edit Contents.

11 Select the handle blend. Choose Effects ➤ Clear Blend. Draw a rectangle whose lower boundary is at the point where the brush handle enters the water. Select the rectangle. In the Intersect Roll-Up, Leave Original Target Object and Leave Original Other Objects ➤ Intersect With. Click one of the brush objects. Repeat for the other handle object. (If you select the rectangle first, then intersect with one of the brush objects, the newly created intersect object will retain the brush color.)

12 Drag the top-middle handle of the rectangle's highlighting box straight down. Intersect again with one of the original handle objects, only this time uncheck Leave Original Target Object. Then, do the other handle object, this last time unchecking both Leave Original Target Object and Leave Original Other Objects.

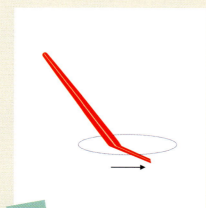

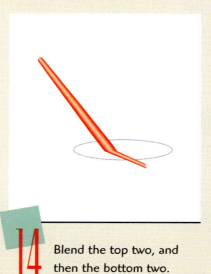

13 You should have four objects left. Select the two lower ones. Click again to bring up the rotate and skew handles. Drag the lower skew handle to the right.

14 Blend the top two, and then the bottom two.

15 Finish Editing This Level.

19

Making Things Move

What you will learn

- Creating blur, strobe, and trailing-highlight motion effects

- Creating motion effects over multicolored backgrounds

- Using efficient object-construction techniques

Portraying motion in a static image is a problem that has often troubled illustrators. Solutions range from symbolic cartoon motion lines to superimposed images. This project will look at three techniques—the motion blur, strobe, and trailing highlights.

The motion blur effect is familiar as a photographic technique, typically created with lengthy exposures. The trick is to create a blur of color behind the object which gradually fades into the background. Blends do the trick.

The implementation of the strobe effect is similar to the blur, only many fewer Blend steps are used. The result is similar to photographic film

exposed with multiple exposures, and works well for intricate objects.

The trailing-highlights technique, frequently used in airbrush renderings, uses a streak of color behind the object.

Creating these motion effects at their most basic is ridiculously easy—four steps for the dart examples shown here, and you're done! The real fun starts when the effect is placed in front of a multicolored background.

Don't overlook the design potential here. The illusion of movement adds dynamic tension to your layouts. Use it to convey excitement, change, or to lead the eye to a key element.

These colors are used in this section.

■ 100%K	■ Blue 100%C, 20%M	■ Yellow 10%K 9%M, 100%Y, 10%K
■ 50%K	■ 30% Blue 30%C, 6%M	■ 30% Yellow 10K 3%M, 30%Y, 3%K	■ Yellow 30%K 9%M, 100%Y, 30%K
■ Dark Gold 25%M, 75%Y, 20%K	■ Green 90%C, 90%Y	■ Yellow 20%K 9%M, 100%Y, 20%K	■ Pink 100%M, 40%Y
■ Light Gold 5%M, 15%Y	■ 30% Green 27%C, 27%Y	■ 30% Yellow 20K 3%M, 30%Y, 6%K	■ Purple 30%C, 76%M, 28%Y

Tips for Drawing Darts

Since this project is about motion effects, drawing the dart will not be explained in great detail. Even though there are a lot of little pieces, it's really a simple thing to draw. The lesson below should be enough to get you through.

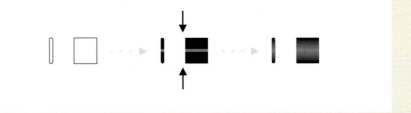

1 The barrel of the dart is constructed from symmetrical objects. The simplest sections are made from rectangles and rounded rectangles. Stretch Vertically to 10%. Apply To Duplicate. Fill the originals with 100%K, and the Duplicates with 60%K. Blend.

2 For the more complex sections, draw the curvature of one side. In the Scale & Mirror page of the Transform Roll-Up, Mirror Vertically. Apply To Duplicate. Move straight down. Select both, and Combine. With the Shape Tool, select two nodes. Then, click the Join With Segment button in the Node Edit Roll-Up. Repeat for the other side. Fill to Dark Gold. Stretch Vertically to 10%. Apply To Duplicate. Fill with Light Gold. Blend the two.

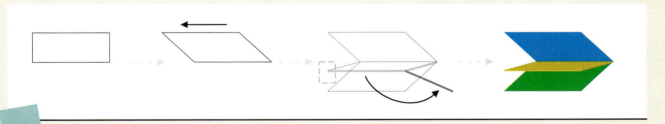

3 For the fins, skew a rectangle. For the leading edge of the yellow fin, duplicate the side of the yellow fin. Convert To Curves. With Snap To Objects on, select the two left nodes. Drag by the top one, rotate around, and snap into place. Fill the top fin with Blue, the middle fin with Yellow 20%K, the side of the yellow fin with Yellow 10%K, the leading edge of the yellow fin with Yellow 30%K, and the bottom fin with Green.

Learning Motion Blur

The motion blur is created by drawing blurs of color behind the moving object. The technique shown here uses CorelDRAW's Blend feature. In some cases, fountain fills can be substituted for blends. They have the advantage of being easier to create, but do not convey the shape of the object being put into motion.

1 Select the three fins, plus the edge of the yellow fin. Duplicate (Plus [+] key on the numeric keypad). Fill each of the duplicates with 30% tints of their respective base colors (30% Blue, 30% Yellow 20K, 30% Yellow 10K, 30% Green).

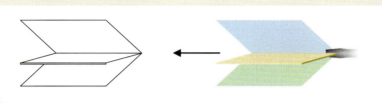

2 Select the four fin objects from the previous step. Drag straight left (hold the Ctrl key to constrain movement). Click the right mouse button to leave the originals. Fill the new objects to the background color (here=White; outlines for clarity only). Send To Back.

3 Select the 30% Blue fin and its White duplicate. Blend. Use plenty of steps so there are no gaps where the background shows through.

4 Create similar blends for the other fin sections. Select the blends, and send To Back.

Using Trailing Highlights

Here's a variation called trailing highlights. It works great for complex objects because you can just create the color streaks for prominent features.

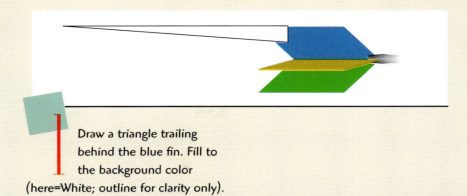

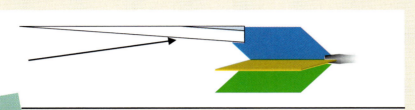

1 Draw a triangle trailing behind the blue fin. Fill to the background color (here=White; outline for clarity only).

2 Drag the lower-left corner handle of the highlighting box up and to the right, clicking the right mouse button to leave the original. Fill to 30% Blue.

3 Blend the two. Send To Back.

4 Repeat for the yellow and green fins, using 30% tints of their respective base colors.

Mastering the Strobe Effect

The trick to the strobe effect is that you need to create a "ghosted" duplicate of the original object, using tints of the original's colors.

Fortunately, CorelDRAW has the unique ability to blend grouped objects, which lends itself to quickly tinting a complex illustration.

1 Select all the dart components, and Group. Move straight left, clicking the right mouse button to leave the original. Fill the duplicate with White. (Outline for clarity only.) Send To Back.

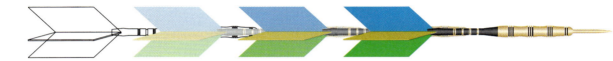

2 Blend in two steps.

3 Separate. Click off the blend to deselect. Click the Blend again, and Ungroup. Delete the second dart from the right. The remaining "ghosted" dart is a 33% tint of the original.

4 Turn on Snap To Objects. Select the middle "ghosted" dart by the top-left node of the blue fin. Drag and snap to the highlighted node on the original. The dart will now be hidden under the original. With it still selected, Shift+click the white dart, and Blend in two steps. The white dart and the ghosted dart directly under the original now serve no purpose, so if you want, Separate the blend and delete them.

Blurring over Colored Backgrounds

The motion effects use blends from the background color to a color that is a mix of the background color and the color of the object in motion. When either the background or the object is white, just mix a tint by taking a percentage of each of the color's CMYK values. The strength of the tint is an artistic decision. In the case of the arrow fins, 30% was used. When neither color is white, you must calculate the "to" color by combining the color values of the motion object and the background. First, decide the relative strength of the effect as a percentage. The strength of the background contribution will be 100% minus that value. Multiply the effect percentage times the CMYK values of the motion object (fin color in this case).

Then, multiply the background contribution times the CMYK values of the background color. Finally, add the two.

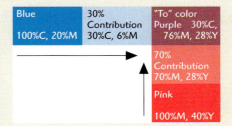

Blue	30%	"To" color
100%C, 20%M	Contribution 30%C, 6%M	Purple 30%C, 76%M, 28%Y

70% Contribution 70%M, 28%Y

Pink 100%M, 40%Y

1 To blur over the pink rectangle, duplicate the original blue blur. Make sure Automatically center new powerclip contents is turned off. PowerClip the duplicated blur into the pink rectangle.

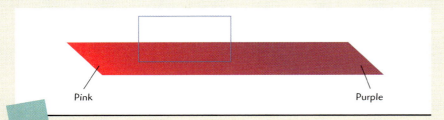

Pink   Purple

2 With the rectangle selected, choose Effects ➢ PowerClip ➢ Edit Contents. The display will show the PowerClipped blend, and the rectangle container outlined in blue. Change the blend "from" color to Pink, and the blend "to" color to Purple. DRAW will automatically reblend with the new colors.

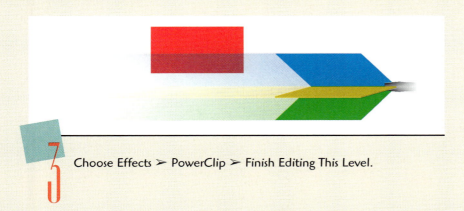

3 Choose Effects ➢ PowerClip ➢ Finish Editing This Level.

Making Things Spin

What you will learn

- Creating spinning blur and strobe effects

- Using nested PowerClips to integrate the blur effect into underlying image details

A nother common type of movement is radial, or spinning, motion. While the same basic principles discussed in the previous project on linear motion apply, some special techniques are required. Blended triangles and nested PowerClips do the trick for a radial motion blur. DRAW's ability to position the center of rotation, and its truly unique transparency lens, make short work of a spinning strobe effect.

IMPORTANT NOTE: For versions 5 and 6 only.

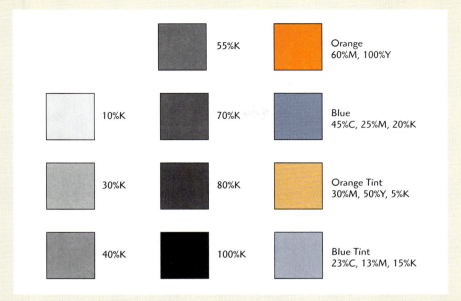

	55%K		Orange 60%M, 100%Y
10%K	70%K		Blue 45%C, 25%M, 20%K
30%K	80%K		Orange Tint 30%M, 50%Y, 5%K
40%K	100%K		Blue Tint 23%C, 13%M, 15%K

These colors are used in this section.

Creating a Speedometer Face

The steps in this exercise should be applicable to many different gauge faces. If you want to duplicate the example, draw a speedometer similar to the one shown, using the fills indicated.

10%K

30%K

Color Limit Lens;
Color: 80%K;
Amount: 15%

70%K

100%K

Orange

Blue

Spinning Blur

Over the speedometer face, Ctrl+Shift+drag a circle from the center of the dial so the circumference is just touching the tip of the speedometer needle (blue outline for clarity only). Draw a triangle, starting from the same center point, through the tip of the speedometer needle, down and to the left to where the motion effect is to begin (staying far enough out so as to clear the circle), and back to the center point.

2 Fill to the background color (70%K, outlines for clarity only). Duplicate (Plus [+] key on the numeric keypad). With the Shape Tool, select the highlighted node. Move up and to the right, along the edge of the original triangle, until only a thin sliver is left. Fill with 40%K, which is a 50% mix of the background color (70%K) and the needle color (10%K). Select the two triangles. Blend.

> **HINT**
>
> If you've used a Color Limit Lens for the needle shadow, the shadow will appropriately interact with the motion blur.

3 Make sure Automatically center new powerclip contents is turned off. Select the blended triangles. PowerClip into the circle from step 1.

4 Select the PowerClip circle and the dial face. Send To Back.

5 With the PowerClip circle selected, Shift+drag the top-left corner handle down and to the right until the circumference of the circle just touches the outer edge of the needle stub. Click the right mouse button to leave the original.

6 Each detail under the blur effect will require a similar treatment. You can simplify things if you select and Combine all underlying features filled with the same color, like the orange objects shown here (outlined in blue for clarity). Select the motion blur. Duplicate (Plus [+] key). PowerClip into the combined orange object.

7 Repeat for the other underlying features—the blue details and the needle hub. Remember to PowerClip both the large and small blurs into the hub. At this point the display will look like you placed the original blur effect in front of all the details.

8 Select each detail in turn, choose Effects ➤ Power-Clip ➤ Edit Contents. Choose the blur effect and Edit Contents again. Change the blend "from" color to the detail's color. Change the "to" color to a 50% mix of the detail's color and 10%K (the needle color). (For the blue details, the "to" color is Blue Tint; for the orange details, use Orange Tint; for the black speedometer hub, use 55%K.) Choose PowerClip ➤ Finish Editing This Level twice.

Spinning Strobe

1 A strobe effect, for simple objects over complex backgrounds, can be quickly created using a Transparency Lens. Turn on Snap To Objects. Select the speedometer needle, and duplicate (Plus [+] key). Click again to bring up the rotate and skew handles. Snap the center of rotation marker to the center of the speedometer. Rotate the speedometer counterclockwise. Apply a Transparency Lens to the speedometer objects. Accept the assigned color (which will be the object's current color); Rate: 75%.

2 Create a second phantom speedometer needle, this time using a Rate of 50%. Select the original needle, and send To Front.

21

Drawing a Box from *Any Angle*

What you will learn

- Knowing the difference between isometric, dimetric, and trimetric drawings

- Manipulating flat panels into three-dimensional boxes

- Shading a box realistically

Starting from easy-to-draw flat panels, this project explains how to draw a box as seen from any point of view. The table on the following page gives values used to manipulate the panels for different elevation and rotation angles. The exercise explains how to calculate these values using the Windows Scientific Calculator.

Most of the table examples are classified as trimetric (3 scales) drawings, with each face shown in a different proportion. Whenever a rotation angle of 45 degrees is used, the front and end panels will be in equal proportion, resulting in a dimetric (2 scales) drawing. For the unique case shown in the bottom row, an isometric (1 scale) drawing will result, with all three faces shown in equal proportion.

	5%K		100%K
	15%K		Red 100%M, 100%Y
	30%K		Blue 10%K 100%C, 50%M, 10%K
	75%K		Blue 25%K 100%C, 50%M, 25%K

These colors are used in this section.

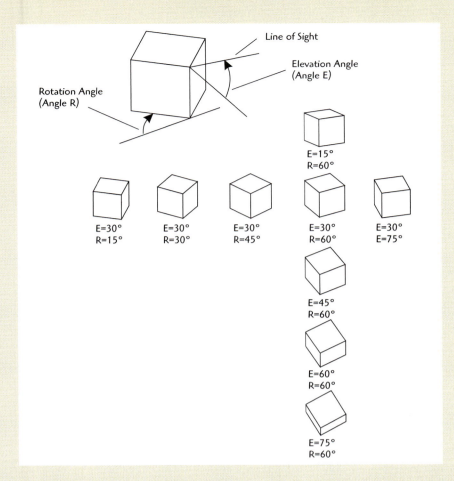

Line of Sight

Elevation Angle
(Angle E)

Rotation Angle
(Angle R)

E=15°
R=60°

E=30°   E=30°   E=30°   E=30°   E=30°
R=15°   R=30°   R=45°   R=60°   E=75°

E=45°
R=60°

E=60°
R=60°

E=75°
R=60°

Table 23.1

Transformation values for different elevation and skew angles

Elevation angle (E), degrees	Roatation angle (R), degrees	Skew angle for end, degrees	Skew angle for front, degrees	Vertical stretch, %	Horizontal stretch for front, %	Horizontal stretch for end, %
15.00	60.00	24.15	8.50	96.59	86.60	50.00
30.00	15.00	7.63	61.81	86.60	25.88	96.59
30.00	30.00	16.10	40.89	86.60	50.00	86.60
30.00	45.00	26.57	26.57	86.60	70.71	70.71
30.00	60.00	40.89	16.10	86.60	86.60	50.00
30.00	75.00	61.81	7.63	86.60	96.59	25.88
45.00	60.00	50.77	22.21	70.71	86.60	50.00
60.00	60.00	56.31	26.57	50.00	86.60	50.00
75.00	60.00	59.13	29.15	25.88	86.60	50.00
35.26	45.00	30.00	30.00	81.65	70.71	70.71

HINT

Use a box of your own shape and design if you want. Note that the height of the top panel must be the same as the width of the end panel, just like a real box. Fill the details of the top panel with your chosen base colors. For proper shading, given a light source from the right and above the box, add 10%K or so to the base colors for the front panel, and 25%K or so to the base colors for the end panel.

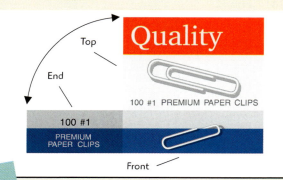

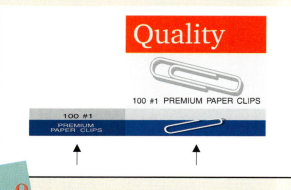

1 Draw and align the top, front, and end panels, as shown. (For the purposes of this exercise, just draw the box without the paper clip if you want.) The following colors were used here: Top panel: Red, 5%K, 75%K; Front panel: Blue 10%K, 15%K; End panel: Blue 25%K, 30%K, 100%K.

2 For this example, an Elevation angle of 50 degrees and a Rotation angle of 55 degrees were chosen. Select the front and end panels. In the Scale & Mirror page of the Transform Roll-Up, click the down arrow and select any of the top row of anchor point checkboxes. Enter V: 64.28% (the cosine of the Elevation angle). Apply.

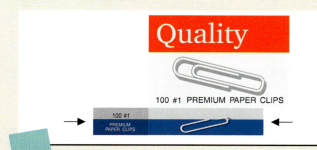

3 With the end panel selected, in the Scale & Mirror page of the Transform Roll-Up select any of the right row of anchor point checkboxes. Enter H: 57.36% (the cosine of the Rotation angle). Apply. (Remember to reset V: to 100%.) With the front panel selected, in Scale & Mirror select any of the left row of anchor points. Enter H: 81.92% (the sine of the Rotation angle). Apply.

HINT

For the technically inclined, here are the mind-boggling details: The end panel is skewed by –arc tangent [(tangent R) (sine E)]. In other words, multiply the tangent of the rotation angle times the sine of the elevation angle. Get the arc tangent of the result. (Typically, to find the arc tangent, press the inv key, then the tan key.) Using the Windows Scientific Calculator, the sequence is: 55, tan, *, 50, sin, =, inv, tan.

The front panel is skewed by the arc tangent [(cotangent R) (sine E)]. The cotangent of R = 1/ tangent R, so use the 1/x key. Using the Windows Scientific Calculator: 55, tan, 1/x, *, 50, sin, =, inv, tan.

4 Select the end panel. In the Skew page of the Transform Roll-Up, click Use Anchor Point. Select any of the right anchor points. Enter V: –47.57. Apply. With the front panel selected, click any of the left anchor points. Enter V: 28.21. Apply.

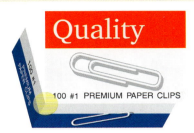

HINT

You can drag a middle handle diagonally to snap to a node. The object will only stretch in one direction (Step 6).

5 Turn on Snap To Objects. Select the front and end panels. Click again to bring up the rotate and skew handles. Drag the center of rotation marker to the highlighted intersection of all three panels. In Rotation in the Transform Roll-Up, enter Angle: –28.21 degrees. Apply. (This is the same value that you skewed the front panel, so if you're making a box with a different viewpoint, use that skew value.)

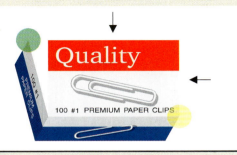

6 Select the top panel. Drag the right-middle handle to the left, then down. Snap to the yellow highlighted node. Drag the top-middle handle down and to the left. Snap to the green highlighted node.

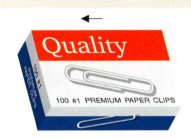

7 Horizontally skew the top panel until it aligns with the end panel. You can zoom in and do this by eye, or, if you prefer, use the Skew page in the Transform Roll-Up (see Hint at right).

HINT

The exact Horizontal skew angle is 90 minus (skew angle for the end panel + skew angle for the front panel). So that would be 90 minus (47.57 + 28.21), which is 14.22. Select any of the lower row of anchor points. Click Apply.

8 Select all, and use Rotation in the Transform Roll-Up to rotate counterclockwise by the same value you used in step 5 (28.21 degrees).

HINT

By varying the elevation and rotation angles, you can dramatically alter the appearance of the box. If you're using this technique to show a product package design to your client, you might want to include several views, each view emphasizing a different side.

Elevation angle=30 degrees
Rotation angle=15 degrees

Elevation angle=60 degrees
Rotation angle=60 degrees

22

Drawing *Anything* from *Any* Angle

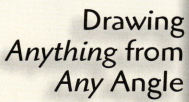

What you will learn

- Manipulating flat panels into three-dimensional cross sections

- Using cross sections to construct a three-dimensional illustration

- Logical shading, from blocking in to detailing

n much the same way that simple rectangular panels can be manipulated into the correct shape and orientation for a three-dimensional box, so can cross-sectional views of more complex objects. These cross sections serve as a skeleton on which to build the illustration. In many cases, details such as the lettering on this scanner are accurate and complete, needing only to be filled with the appropriate color. In other cases, notably sections that curve off the cross-sectional plane, only partial outlines can be provided. Nevertheless, these serve as crucial building blocks for the final details.

The first example explains how to draw a hand scanner using horizontal cross sections. The second example looks at a similar situation using vertical cross sections to illustrate a plug.

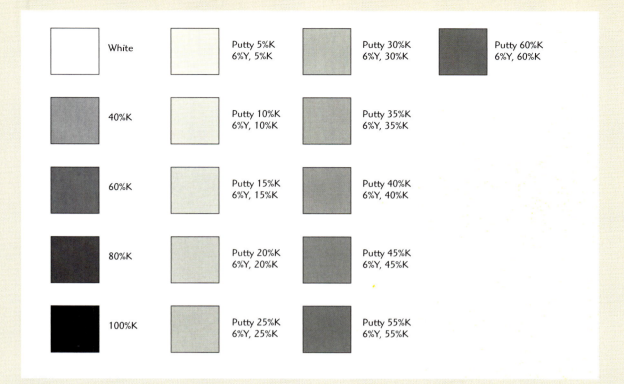

White	Putty 5%K 6%Y, 5%K	Putty 30%K 6%Y, 30%K	Putty 60%K 6%Y, 60%K
40%K	Putty 10%K 6%Y, 10%K	Putty 35%K 6%Y, 35%K	
60%K	Putty 15%K 6%Y, 15%K	Putty 40%K 6%Y, 40%K	
80%K	Putty 20%K 6%Y, 20%K	Putty 45%K 6%Y, 45%K	
100%K	Putty 25%K 6%Y, 25%K	Putty 55%K 6%Y, 55%K	

These colors are used in this section.

Constructing Cross Sections

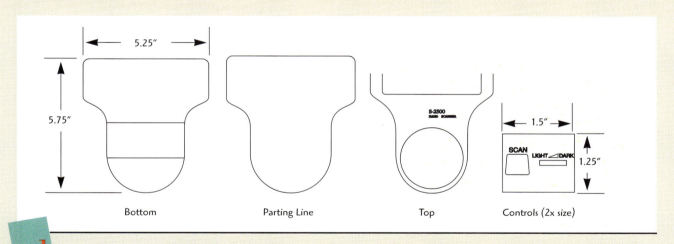

Bottom Parting Line Top Controls (2x size)

Construct accurate outlines for all changes in cross section, plus all horizontally oriented features, as they would appear looking down on the top of the object. Here are outlines for the bottom and top of the scanner, and the parting line where the two plastic halves of the scanner meet. The bottom has two horizontal lines, 1.5 inches apart, which will be used to locate the scanner controls (more on that later). Draw the scanner controls. Place in a box 1.5 inches wide by 1.25 inches high (the height of the scanner). For easy selection later on, Group the controls box, and each cross section.

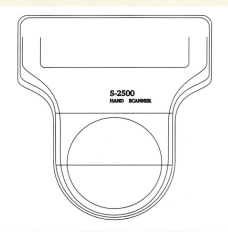

2 Align the three cross sections as if you were looking straight down on the top of the scanner.

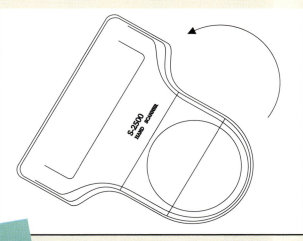

3 The viewpoint for constructing this illustration was chosen with a rotation angle of 60 degrees counterclockwise (CCW), and an elevation angle of 30 degrees. Rotate the cross sections 60 degrees CCW.

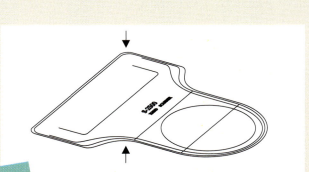

4 In the Scale & Mirror page of the Transform Roll-Up, stretch Vertically to 50% (the sine of the elevation angle).

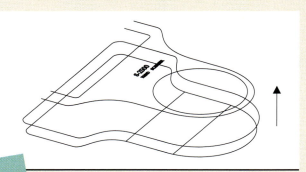

5 Use the Position page in the Transform Roll-Up to move the cross section representing the parting line .325 inches vertically. Move the cross section of the top of the scanner vertically 1.082 inches. (See Hint at right.)

HINT

For different elevation angles, use the Windows Scientific Calculator, enter the value of the angle, click on the sin key.

HINT

Move each cross section vertically by the cosine of the elevation angle multiplied by its true horizontal position relative to the base. In this example, the parting line between the two plastic halves of the scanner is really .375 inches above the bottom of the scanner. The cosine of 30 degrees is .866. The cross section representing the parting line is moved .866 x .375 inches = .325 inches. The scanner is 1.25 inches thick. The cross section of the top of the scanner is moved .866 x 1.25 inches = 1.082 inches.

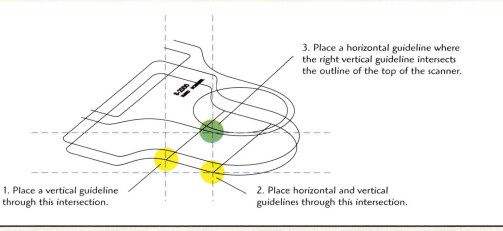

3. Place a horizontal guideline where the right vertical guideline intersects the outline of the top of the scanner.

1. Place a vertical guideline through this intersection.

2. Place horizontal and vertical guidelines through this intersection.

6 That's really all there is to constructing a wire frame for objects that can be defined by horizontal cross sections. In this case, however, the controls box still needs to be positioned. With Snap To Objects on, snap two vertical guidelines to the nodes highlighted in yellow. Snap a horizontal guideline to the lower-right node. Pull in a second horizontal guideline where this vertical guideline intersects the top cross section (green highlight).

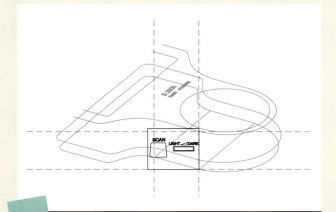

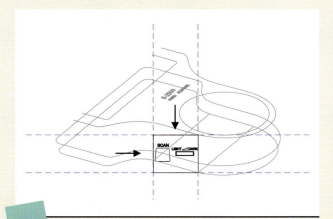

7 With Snap To Guidelines on, snap the outline of the controls box to the right and bottom guidelines.

8 Drag the top-middle handle down. Snap to the top guideline. Drag the left-middle handle to the right. Snap to the left guideline.

9 Double-click the controls box to bring up the rotate and skew handles. Drag the left skew handle up until the top and bottom edges of the controls box align with the top and bottom outlines of the scanner.

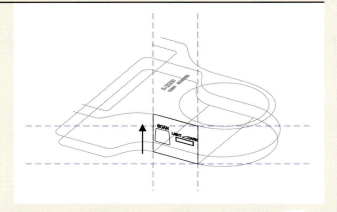

Blocking In

To get a feeling for the appropriate color values, the next stage is to construct and fill objects that define the shape of the scanner. The intention is to block in the overall shape and appropriate tonal values as a basis for further refinement later.

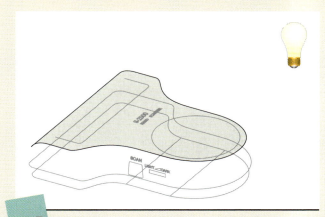

1 Since the front of the scanner is curved, its complete shape could not be included in any of the cross sections. These cross sections do provide a great starting point though. Select and Ungroup the top cross section. Duplicate the outline of the scanner. With the rest of the cross sections for reference, use the Beziér Tool to add and close the curved front. Fill to Putty 15%K.

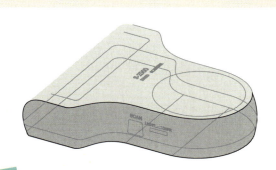

2 Select and Ungroup the bottom cross section. Duplicate both the top and bottom outlines, to be used as the basis for the side of the scanner. Use the Knife Tool to cut the outlines at the appropriate locations. Delete the unnecessary sections. Select and Combine the remaining two sections. Use the Beziér Tool to close the object. Fill with Putty 35%K.

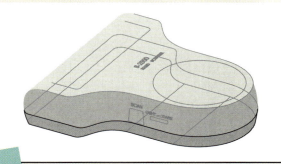

3 Use the same technique to construct the lower side of the scanner, using the bottom and middle cross sections. Fill to Putty 40%K.

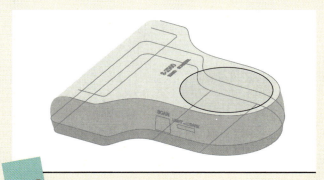

4 Fill the top ellipse to Putty 20%K.

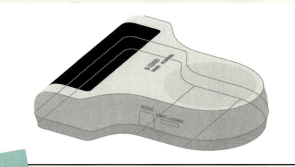

5 Complete the top black plastic section, using the same method as step 1. Fill to 100%K.

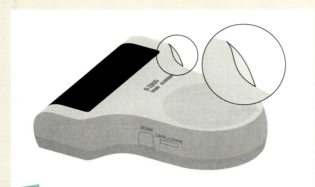

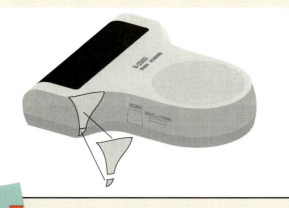

In the Layers Roll-Up, create a new, invisible layer. Move the original cross sections to this layer for safekeeping. Use the Beziér Tool to draw the shape shown. Fill to Putty 10%K.

Shading and Details

At this stage, the basic scanner shape is fairly well defined, and appropriate tonal values have been established for the invented light source. It's time to add detail and subtle shading.

There's a small triangular-shaped section on the shadow side of the scanner that catches some direct light. Use the Beziér Tool to draw the two objects shown. Fill the top one with Putty 20%K, and the bottom with Putty 25%K.

HINT

The edge where the top and side of the scanner meet is rounded, not sharp. It's critical to blend the tonal change between them (step 2 below). Once you do that, there is a problem area where that blend meets the highlight from step 7 in the Blocking In section (step 3-following page).

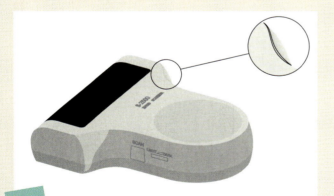

Duplicate the object from step 6 in the Blocking In section. Use the Shape Tool to change to a sliver of the original. Fill to Putty 20%K. Select the two, and Blend.

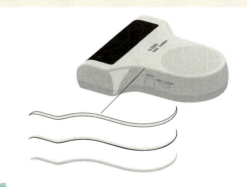

Use the Beziér Tool to draw an object that overlaps the junction between the top and sides of the scanner. Fill to Putty 15%K (the same as the top of the scanner). Duplicate (Plus [+] key). Use the Shape Tool to modify the top part of the outline only, until a sliver of the original is left. Fill with Putty 35%K (the same as the side of the scanner). Select the two, and Blend.

3 Duplicate the blend. Zoom in and change the "from" color to Putty 15%K, and the "to" color to Putty 20%K. DRAW will automatically reblend with the new colors. Draw the object shown (outline for clarity only). Select the blend, and PowerClip into this new object. Assign a fill and outline of none.

4 The ellipse on the scanner top is really a slightly domed area, and so it casts a very thin shadow. Select it, and duplicate. Drag down and to the left slightly. Send Back One. Fill to Putty 30%K.

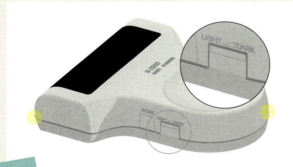

5 Duplicate the original ellipse. Drag one of the corner handles to stretch it way down. Drag it to the approximate location shown. Fill to Putty 5%K. Shift+select the original ellipse. Blend.

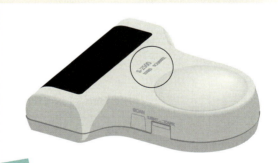

6 To draw the parting line, start by duplicating the bottom side section. Use the Knife Tool to cut at the highlighted locations. Using the Shape Tool and the Node Edit Roll-Up, add nodes and reshape around the brightness intensity knob. In the Outline Pen dialog box, assign the following values: Color: Putty 60%K; Stretch: 20%; Angle: -30 degrees. For this size image, assign about a 2.5-point line width.

7 Select the lettering on the top of the scanner. Fill to 60%K, no outline.

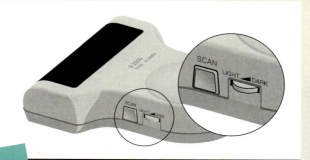

8 Select the lettering on the side of the scanner. Fill to 80%K. Select the button and assign a .5-point, 100%K outline. Fill with a Two Color Linear Fountain Fill: Angle: 45; From: Putty 55%K; To: Putty 20%K. Fill the triangle and rectangle with 100%K.

9 Select and duplicate the button. Drag one of the corner handles to stretch down slightly. Drag down and to the left, as shown. Fill with a Two Color Linear Fountain Fill, using the same colors as the original but change the angle to -135 degrees. Draw the top and side of the brightness knob. Fill the top to Putty 20%K. Fill the side with a Two Color Linear Fountain Fill: Angle: 0; From: Putty 45%K; To: Putty 20%K.

HINT

An intense glare on the black section will render it in shiny plastic. This serves in contrast to the rest of the scanner, which has a rough finish, and therefore a consistent tonal value to each surface.

10 Change the fill of the black cover to a Custom Linear Fountain Fill: Angle: 131; Edge pad: 45%; Position 0%: 100%K; Position 50%: White; Position 100%: 100%K.

11 Retrieve the bottom cross section from the hidden layer. Fill with 40%K. Send To Back. Drag to the left, clicking the right mouse button to leave the original. Fill to White. Send To Back. Blend the two.

HINT

For a discussion of techniques for creating shadows, see Project 16.

Constructing Wire Frames Using Vertical Cross Sections

Borrowing from the previous project on drawing boxes, objects that are better defined using vertical cross sections can also be easily constructed. Cross-sectional views, as many as needed to define the object, are all manipulated just like one side of the box. The other side of the box has vertical lines placed where the cross sections are to be aligned. Once all the objects are transformed, the cross sections are snapped into place, and extraneous lines are deleted.

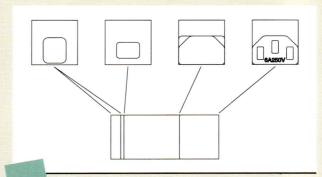

1 Draw all necessary cross sections. Align and group within boxes. Draw a side panel. Place lines to mark the location where each cross section is to be located.

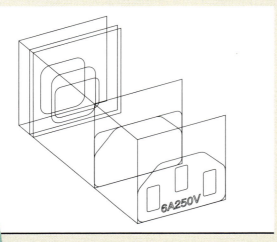

2 Transform each cross section just like the front panels in the box project. Transform the alignment panel like the end panel in the box project. With Snap To Objects on, snap each cross section to the appropriate line.

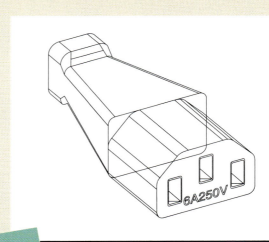

3 Ungroup and delete the boxes. Use the remaining cross sections as a framework to construct the object.

4 The finished plug is really constructed from many simple adjacent shapes. Angled Linear Fountain Fills are used for the rounded corners. Edge-pad and angle values were set as required to ensure a smooth transition between adjacent shades.

23

Putting Things in Perspective

What you will learn

- Understanding the difference between 1-, 2-, and 3-point perspectives

- Laying out a perspective drawing

- Using the Perspective feature to map flat art onto a perspective layout

CorelDRAW's Add Perspective command is an exciting feature which can be used to create technically correct 3-point-perspective illustrations, such as the children's blocks shown here. To understand the difference between 1-, 2-, and 3-point perspectives, refer to the graphics on the next page.

The construction of a perspective drawing is generally described as the projection of an object onto a picture plane. Suppose you're looking out a window at a tree. If you take a marker and trace the outline of the tree on the window, the drawing will show where the light reflecting off the tree and into your eye intersects the window. In this case, the window is the picture plane and the drawing shows the tree's projection onto the picture plane. This basic concept will be used to construct the drawing of children's blocks.

First, you'll construct a simple box in perspective. Then, using a method similar to the one in Project 22, you'll place cross sections within the box to locate the outlines of the blocks. Finally, you'll "apply" the faces to the blocks.

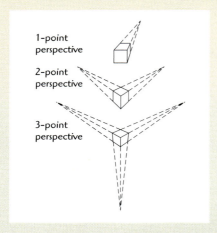

1-point
perspective

2-point
perspective

3-point
perspective

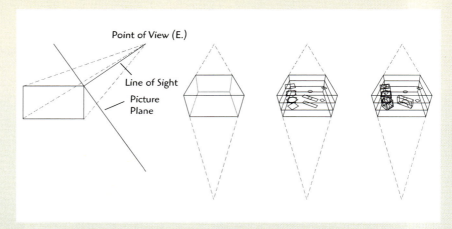

Point of View (E.)

Line of Sight

Picture
Plane

Laying Out a Perspective Drawing

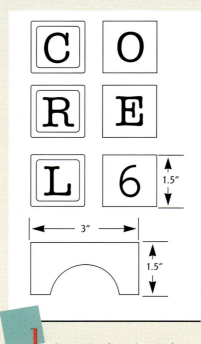

1.5"

3"

1.5"

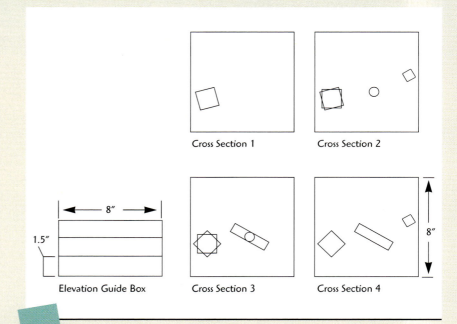

Cross Section 1

Cross Section 2

Elevation Guide Box

Cross Section 3

Cross Section 4

8"

1.5"

8"

1 Draw the face details for the blocks as shown. In the Layers Roll-Up, create a new invisible layer named Blocks. Move these objects to the Blocks layer for safekeeping.

2 Draw cross sections defining the shape and placement of the blocks at ground level, and at the top of each block. These are labeled Cross Section 1 through 4, 4 being the base and 1 the top of the highest block. Group each cross section within a square boundary box.

The Elevation Guide Box is used to locate these horizontal cross sections. This box is the same width as the cross sections, with horizontal lines placed at the correct heights for one, two, or three blocks. Create a new, invisible layer called CrossX. Move the cross sections to this layer, then copy the Elevation Guide Box to it.

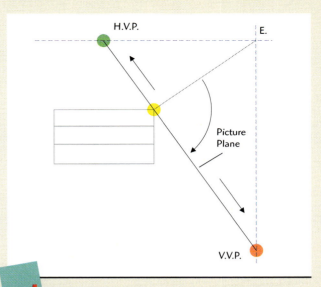

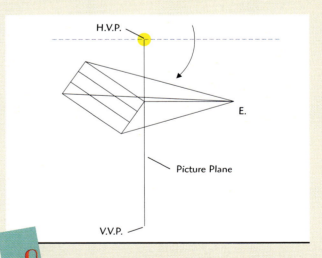

3 Back on Layer 1, choose the observer's point of view (Point E, for "eye"), and crisscross two guidelines at that point. Here, a distance of 10 inches from the top corner of the Elevation Guide Box at an angle of 35 degrees was chosen. With Snap To Objects and Snap To Guidelines on, draw a straight line from Point E to the top-front corner of the box. This is the Line of Sight.

4 Double-click on the line drawn in step 3, and move the center of rotation marker to the left end of the line (yellow highlight). In the Rotate page of the Transform Roll-Up, rotate the line –90 degrees. Apply To Duplicate. Drag the top-left handle of the highlighting box up and to the left, snapping to the green highlight at the horizontal guideline. This point represents the Horizontal Vanishing Point (H.V.P.). Drag the bottom-right handle down and to the right, snapping to the orange highlight, which is the Vertical Vanishing Point (V.V.P.). The line represents the Picture Plane, which is usually constructed perpendicular to the Line of Sight.

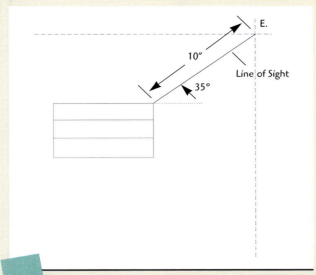

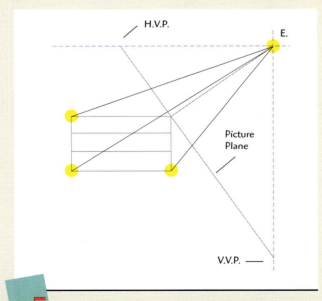

5 Add lines from the other three corners of the box to Point E.

6 Remove the vertical guideline. Select All. Click again to bring up the rotate and skew handles. Move the center of rotation marker to the H.V.P. (yellow highlight), and rotate clockwise by the elevation angle, in this case, –35 degrees. This makes the Picture Plane vertical.

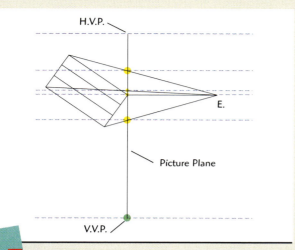

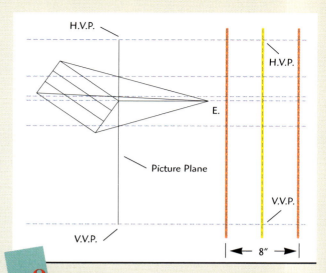

7 Drag in four horizontal guidelines at the yellow highlighted intersections between the Picture Plane and the lines from the corners of the box to Point E. (These locate the projection on the Picture Plane of the Elevation Guide Box.) Snap a horizontal guideline to the green highlighted point (V.V.P.).

8 Pull in a vertical guideline to the right of the drawing (yellow highlight). Pull in two guidelines (orange highlights) centered around the previous guideline and as far apart as the cross section boxes in step 2 are wide (8 inches). Note that the H.V.P. and the V.V.P. have been transferred to the right-side view.

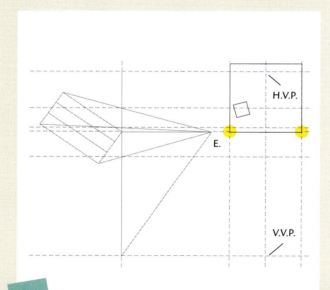

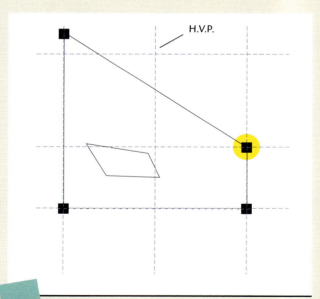

9 Retrieve Cross Section 1 from the CrossX layer. Align the bottom edge with the horizontal guideline through Point E, and the left and right edges with the vertical guidelines from step 8 (yellow highlights).

10 Zoom in. Choose Effects ➢ Add Perspective. Snap the top-right handle to the highlighted guideline intersection.

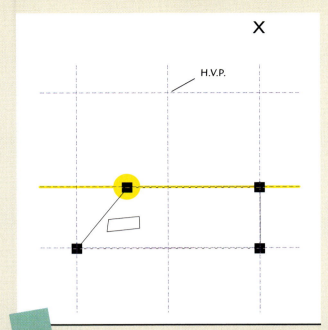

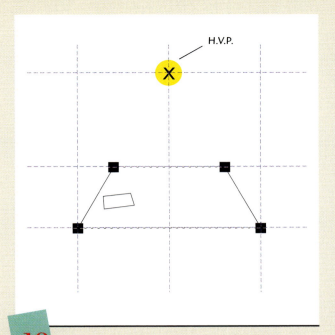

11 Snap the top-left handle to the highlighted horizontal guideline. Move the handle to the right until the Vanishing Point (x) appears on the screen.

12 Snap the vanishing point to the highlighted guideline intersection (H.V.P.).

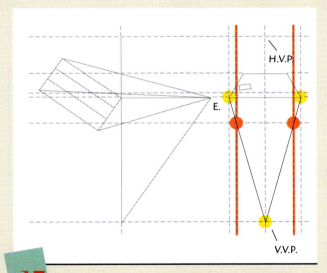

13 Draw lines from the yellow highlighted points to the Vertical Vanishing Point. Zoom in and drag vertical guidelines to the orange highlighted intersections between these lines and the horizontal guideline.

HINT

For a better understanding of why this technique works, carefully study the construction in the next few steps. In step 13, note that the front edge of the cross section on the right view is aligned with the point where the edge of the Elevation Guide Box touches the Picture Plane in the left view. The back edge of this cross section in the right view is aligned where the back edge of the Elevation Guide Box projects onto the Picture Plane in the left view. The left and right sides of this cross section, if extended, would meet at the H.V.P. Neat!

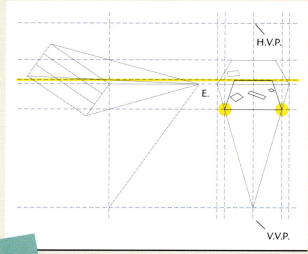

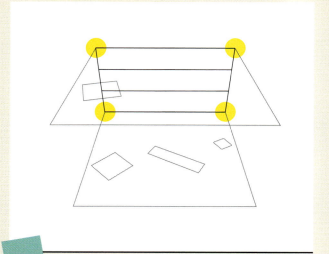

14 Retrieve Cross Section 4 from the CrossX layer. Align the bottom edge to the horizontal guideline, as shown. Add Perspective and proceed as before, aligning the bottom two handles to the highlighted guideline intersections, the top two handles to the highlighted horizontal guideline, and the vanishing point to the H.V.P.

15 At this point, you can delete all guidelines and the lines from step 13. Retrieve a copy of the Elevation Guide Box. Duplicate it (Plus [+] key). Select one copy, and Add Perspective. Snap the four handles, one by one, to the highlighted points.

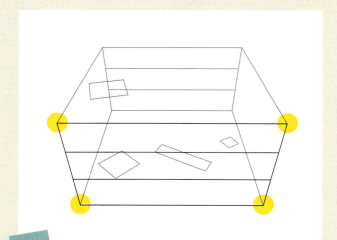

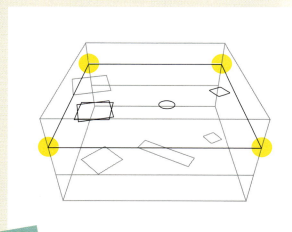

16 Select the other copy of the Elevation Guide Box. Add Perspective. Snap the four handles to the highlighted points.

17 Retrieve Cross Section 2, and repeat using the indicated locations.

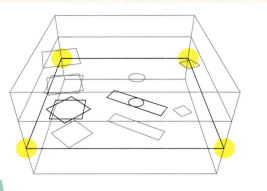

 18 One more time with Cross Section 3.

Adding Flat Art

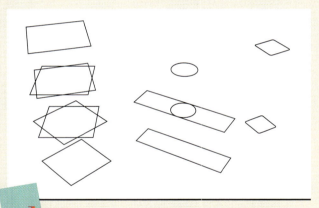

1 Ungroup all elements, and delete the boundary boxes and the Elevation Guide Boxes.

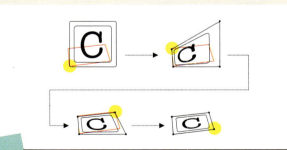

2 Retrieve the letter C face from the Blocks layer. Add Perspective, and snap each handle, one at a time, to the appropriate nodes until all four corners are matched up.

HINT

This method can be modified to construct a 2-point-perspective drawing, as shown here. The picture plane is represented by a vertical line touching the front face of the Elevation Guide Box. There is no vertical vanishing point. The construction is simplified in that steps 4, 6, and 13 are eliminated.

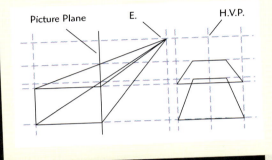

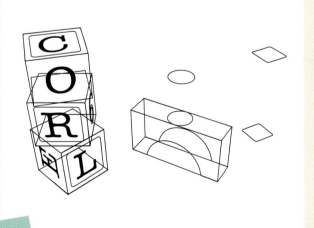

3 Apply the other faces in the same manner.

The coffee illustration was constructed in much the same way as the children's blocks. As shown here, the perspective cross sections are defined, and the lid and labels have been applied in proper perspective. The illustration was completed using the cross–section contours as a guide.

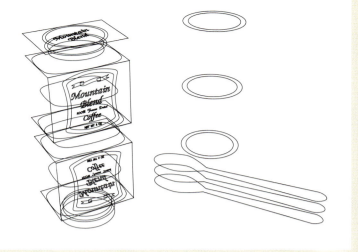

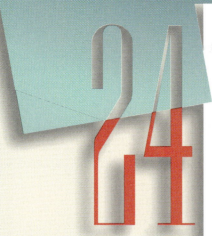

24

Using the Chisel/Bevel Effect with Corel Photo-Paint

What you will learn

- Chiseling and beveling text in Corel Photo-Paint

Corel Photo-Paint can be used to take CorelDRAW artwork to new levels. Here we will use artwork created in previous projects to create valuable effects in Corel Photo-Paint.

IMPORTANT NOTE: Although Corel Photo-Paint became available in CorelDRAW 3, Transparency Masks were not introduced until version 5, and Alpha Channel support is new to version 6.

1 Begin with some text created using the techniques demonstrated in Project 14. Draw a black rectangle or box around the chiseled text. Send the rectangle to the back. Center the text within the rectangle.

2 Fill the top and bottom bevels of the chiseled text as indicated above. Fill the top bevels with a Linear Fountain Fill: From: 50% Black; To: 10% Black; Angle: 180 degrees. Fill the bottom bevels with a Linear Fountain Fill: From: 50% Black; To: 10% Black; Angle: 0 degrees.

Top
Linear Fountain Fill
From: 50% black
To: 10% black
Angle: 180 degrees

Bottom
Linear Fountain Fill
From: 50% black
To: 10% black
Angle: 0 degrees

3 Fill the left and right bevels of the chiseled text as indicated above. Fill the left bevels with a Linear Fountain Fill: From: 50% Black; To: 10% Black; Angle: 90 degrees. Fill the right bevels with a Linear Fountain Fill: From: 50% Black; To: 10% Black; Angle: -90 degrees.

Left
Linear Fountain Fill
From: 50% black
To: 10% black
Angle: 90 degrees

Right
Linear Fountain Fill
From: 50% black
To: 10% black
Angle: -90 degrees

4 Fill any circular shapes such as a C or an O using the Custom Radial Fountain Fill shading principles demonstrated in Project 14. Use the values indicated here for the outer and inner bevels.

Custom Radial Fountain Fill
Horizontal: -38%
Vertical: 15%
60% Black at Position 0%
50% Black at Position 50%
10% Black at Position 100%

Same except
Horizontal: 38%
Vertical: -15%

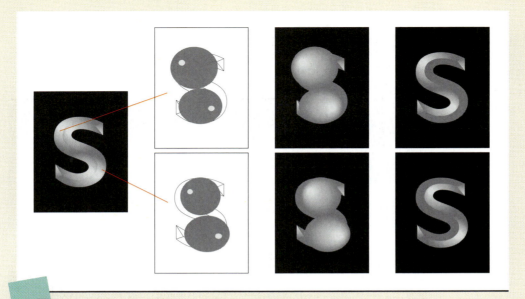

5 Fill any complex shapes, such as an S, using blended ellipses and/or blended triangles, as shown in the section on shading principles in Project 14. Fill the bevels with 50% Gray. Blend between the ellipses and/or triangles from 50% Gray to 10% Gray.

6 Save the chiseled letters and black background in a familiar directory with a name like CHISEL.CDR, or perhaps with something more descriptive in Win95 such as CHISEL EFFECT.CDR.

7 Send everything but the top-oriented segments to the back. Leave the right segments of any curved objects in front, such as C and S in this example. Choose Save As from the File menu. Save the file as TOP.CDR.

8 Send everything but the bottom-oriented segments to the back. Leave the left segments of any curved objects in front, such as C and S in this example. Choose Save As from the File menu. Save the file as BOTTOM.CDR.

9 Send everything but the left-oriented segments to the back. Choose Save As from the File menu. Save the file as LEFT.CDR.

10 Send everything but the right-oriented segments to the back. Choose Save As from the File menu. Save the file as RIGHT.CDR.

1 Open Corel Photo-Paint. Create a document the same size as the black rectangle you created in CorelDRAW. Fill the document with a texture, such as granite, or one of Photo-Paint's texture fills. This example used a granite texture from the Textures II Corel Professional Photos CD-ROM. The granite texture was opened at Poster size (2048x3072), then cropped with the Paper Size feature to 6.75 inches wide by 2 inches high.

To quickly test this technique, make the resolution of the texture document in Corel Photo-Paint RGB 72 dpi. For offset printing, CMYK 300 dpi is preferable; but for a quick test, 72 is faster.

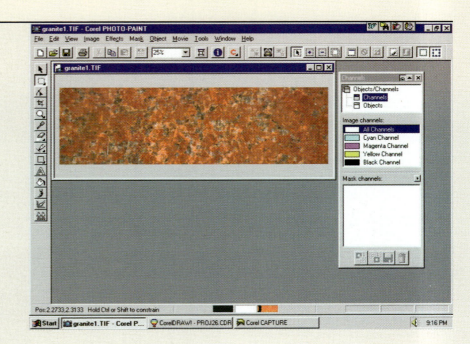

HINT

Corel Photo-Paint 6 uses Channels instead of Transparency Masks as in Corel Photo-Paint 5. Nevertheless, both only use 256 levels of gray in the Channel/Transparency Mask. Choosing anything more than 256 levels of gray is a wasted effort. Also, make sure the Anti-aliasing feature is off, or you will lose some parts of the Channel or Transparency Mask.

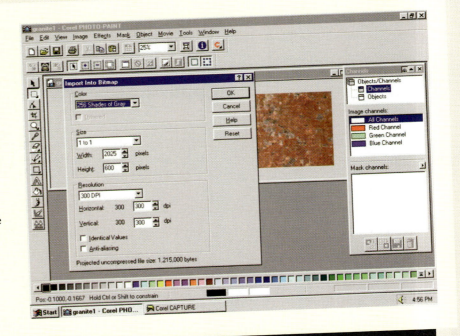

12 Open the Channels Roll-Up (Ctrl+F9). Click on the little triangle to the right of the Mask channels box header. Open TOP.CDR in the same resolution that you chose for the texture file. Once the TOP.CDR Mask Channel is loaded, click on the first button on the left under the Mask channels section of the Channels Roll-Up. From Effects ➢ Color Adjust, select the Brightness-Contrast-Intensity filter. Apply the filter with a brightness of 60. Remove the mask by selecting None from the Mask menu. Select the channel created by TOP.CDR. Click on the trash can to delete it.

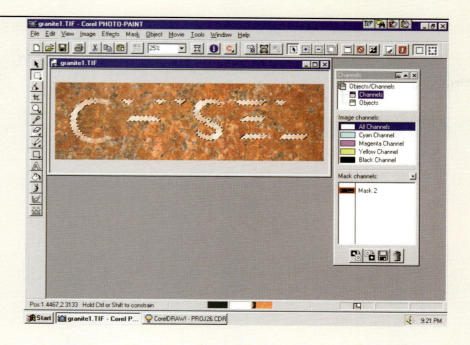

13 Open BOTTOM.CDR as a Mask Channel. Load the Mask Channel as a Mask by clicking on the first button on the left under the Mask channels section of the Channels Roll-Up. From Effects ➢ Color Adjust, select the Brightness-Contrast-Intensity filter. Apply the filter with a brightness of –60 (note the negative value). Remove the mask. Delete the channel.

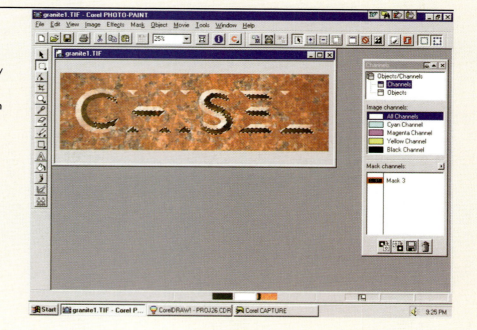

14 Open LEFT.CDR as a Mask Channel. Load the Mask Channel as a Mask. From Effects ➢ Color Adjust, select the Brightness-Contrast-Intensity filter. Apply the filter with a brightness of 40. Remove the mask. Delete the channel.

15 Open RIGHT.CDR as a Mask Channel. Load the Mask Channel as a Mask. From Effects ➢ Color Adjust, select the Brightness-Contrast-Intensity filter. Apply the filter with a brightness of –40 (note the negative value). Remove the mask. Delete the channel.

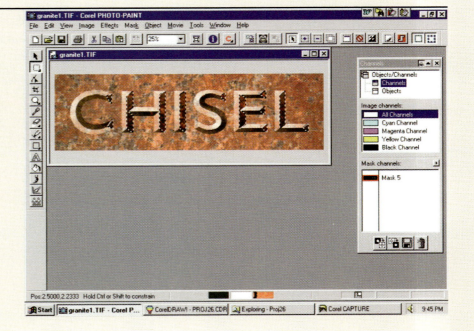

This technique can also be used in conjunction with the bevels demonstrated in Project 7. In this example, the custom bevel shapes were utilized to create the impression that NAP Marketing Inc.'s beveled logo is being gradually chiseled away.

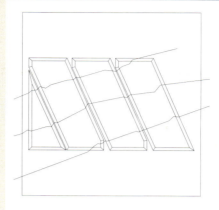
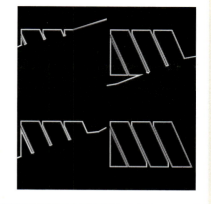

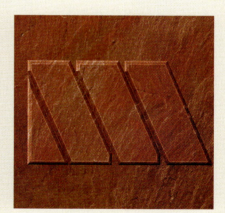

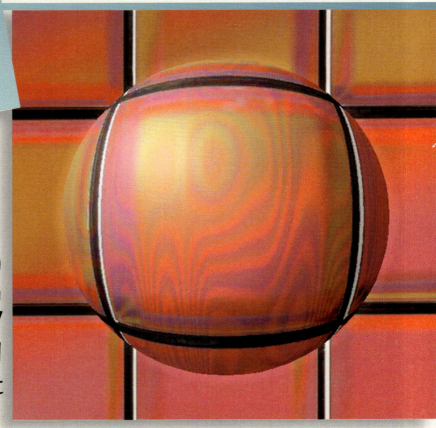

Building Custom Masks in CorelDRAW and Corel Photo-Paint

What you will learn

- Rendering bubbles with Corel Photo-Paint

- Rendering buttons with Corel Photo-Paint

ustom fountain fills such as those demonstrated in Project 9 can be used as Alpha Channels or Transparency Masks to create interesting effects. While Dream 3D may be better at creating three-dimensional circle effects with bitmapped textures, Photo-Paint can be used to render photorealistic bubbles.

IMPORTANT NOTE: Although Corel Photo-Paint became available in CorelDRAW 3, Transparency Masks were not introduced until version 5, and Alpha Channel support is new to version 6.

Rendering Bubbles

1 Begin by centering a 1.5-inch circle within a 2-inch square. Fill the circle with 90% Black, and the square with 100% Black. Make sure the circle is in front of the square and remove the outline. Save the file as BUB-MASK1.CDR.

2 Create a duplicate of the circle and square. Fill the circle with a Custom Radial Fountain Fill with the following colors in the positions indicated in the Color Blend section of the Custom Radial Fill dialog box: Position 0%: 100% Black; Position 50%: 100% Black; Position 60%: 80% Black; Position 85%: 30% Black; Position 95%: White; Position 100%: White. Adjust the Center offset to Horizontal –20% and Vertical 20%. Change the number of Steps to 256. (Note: this is located in the Options section of the Fountain Fill dialog box. The default is 20 steps. The Steps option is grayed out until you press on the small "lock" button.) Leave the square black. Select only the newly duplicated circle and square, and choose Save As from the File menu. Check the Selected Only box, and save the file as BUB-MASK2.CDR.

3 Create another duplicate of the circle and square. Fill the circle with a Custom Radial Fountain Fill with the following colors in the positions indicated in the Color Blend section of the Custom Radial Fill dialog box: Position 0%: White; Position 20%: White; Position 25%: 30% Black; Position 40%: 60% Black; Position 50%: 100% Black; Position 100%: 100% Black. Adjust the Center offset to Horizontal 20% and Veritcal 20%. Change the number of Steps to 256. Leave the square black. Select only

the newly duplicated circle and square, and choose Save As from the File menu. Check the Selected Only box, and save the file as BUB-MASK3.CDR.

4 Create another duplicate of the circle and square. Fill the circle with White. Press the Plus (+) key to create a duplicate. Then, cut the duplicate to the clipboard. Open the Contour Roll-Up. Change the settings to Outside, Offset .05, Steps 1. Click Apply. Separate and Ungroup the new circle. Remove the outline, and change the fill to Black. Select the two circles. Blend between them with 40 steps. Paste the duplicate circle back into the file, and fill with Black. Leave the square black. Select only the newly created circles and square, and choose Save As from the File menu. Check the Selected Only box, and save the file as BUB-MASK4.CDR.

5 Create another duplicate of the circle and square. Fill the circle with White. Leave the square black. Select only the newly created circles and square, and choose Save As from the File menu. Check the Selected Only box, and save the file as BUBMASK5.CDR.

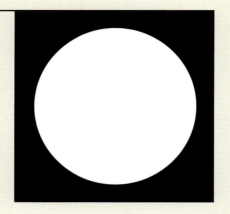

6 Open Corel Photo-Paint. Create a new image that is 2 inches square at your preferred resolution. Fill the document with a texture or background, such as tile. This example was created with a tile image from PhotoDisc's Volume 8 Backgrounds and Objects. The tile background was resampled and cropped to 2 inches square. Once you have a background, open the Channels Roll-Up. Click Mask Channels ➢ Open. Then, from Load a Mask from Disk, choose BUB-MASK1.CDR. Select Mask ➢ Mode ➢ Normal (Ctrl+1).

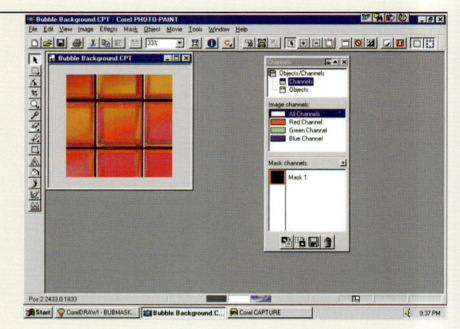

7 Select Mask ➣ Load, and select the channel you just opened. Or, click on the bottom-left button in the Channels Roll-Up to load the channel as a mask. Apply a colorful texture such as those created by Kai's Power Tools Texture Explorer or one of Corel Photo-Paint's custom Texture fills. Remove the mask by selecting None from the Mask menu. Delete the channel by clicking on the Mask in the Roll-Up, and then clicking on the Trash Can.

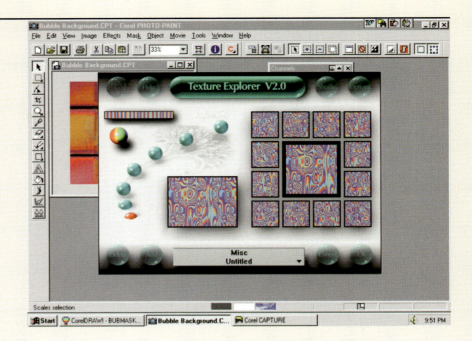

8 Open BUBMASK5.CDR as a channel. Load the channel as a mask, as in step 6 above. From Effects ➣ 3D Effects, select the Map to Object effect. Apply the effect with a Spherical Mapping mode at 20%. Remove the mask and delete the channel, as in the preceding step.

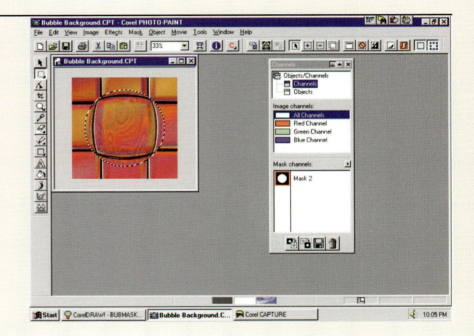

9 Open BUBMASK2.CDR as a channel. Load the channel as a mask, as in step 6 above. Select Effects ➤ Color Adjust ➤ Brightness-Contrast-Intensity effect. Apply it with a brightness of 40. Remove the mask and delete the channel, as in step 7 above.

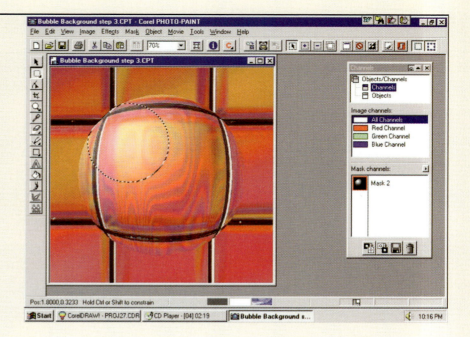

10 Open BUBMASK3.CDR as a channel. Load the channel as a mask, as in step 6 above. Select the Brightness-Contrast-Intensity effect. Apply it with a brightness of –40. Remove the mask and delete the channel, as in step 7 above.

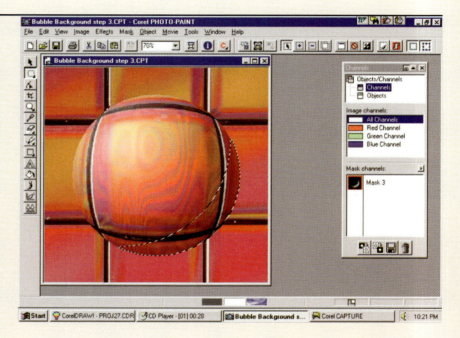

11 Open BUBMASK4.CDR as a channel. Load the channel as a mask, as in step 6. Select the Brightness-Contrast-Intensity effect. Apply it with a brightness of 7. Remove the mask and delete the channel, as in step 7.

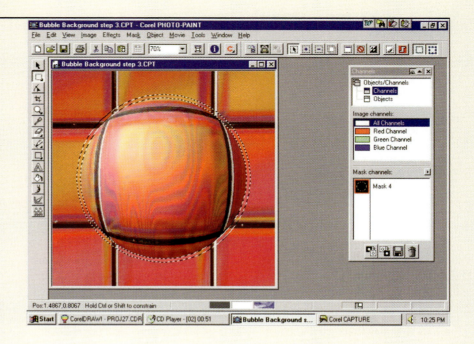

12 Multiple bubbles can be created in the same way. All of the steps, except the Map to Object filter step, can be applied with any number of bubbles. Each individual bubble, however, will have to have the Map to Object filter applied separately.

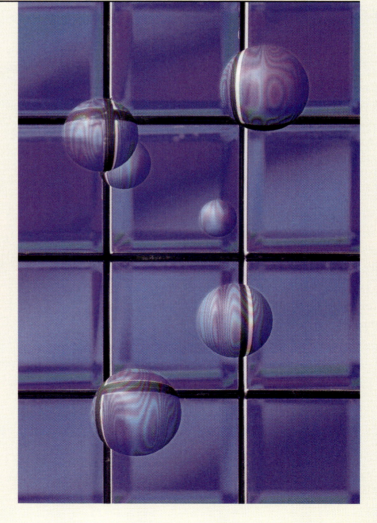

Rendering Buttons

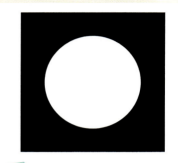

1 Buttons can easily be rendered with a similar approach. Draw a 1-inch circle and a 1.5-inch square. Fill the square with Black, and the circle with a Linear Fountain Fill from Black to White at 135 degrees with 256 steps. Remove the outline.

2 Open the Scale Transform Roll-Up (Alt+F9). Change the Horizontal and Vertical scales to 80%. Click on the Apply To Duplicate button. Save the file as BUTTON1a.CDR.

3 Delete the center duplicate circle. Fill the remaining circle with White. Save the file as BUTTON1b.CDR.

4 Open Corel Photo-Paint. Create a document that is 1.5 inches square at your preferred resolution. Fill the document with a texture or background. This example was created with the Stucco Texture fill from Corel Photo-Paint's Sample texture library. Once you have a background, open the Channels Roll-Up. Open BUTTON1a.CDR as a channel. Load the channel as a mask. Apply the Brightness-Contrast-Intensity effect with a brightness of 50.

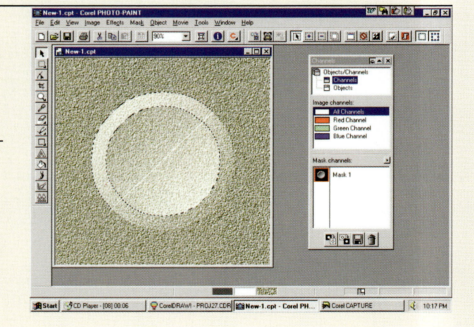

5 Select Invert from the Mask menu. Apply the Brightness–Contrast–Intensity effect with a brightness of 50. Remove the mask. Delete the channel.

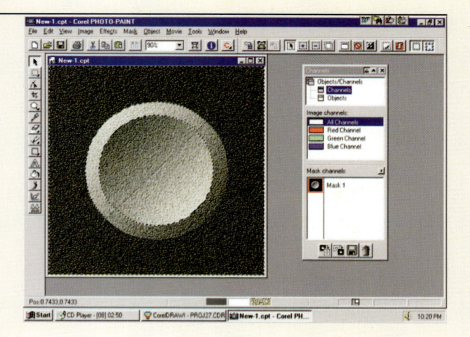

6 Open BUTTON1b.CDR as a channel. Load the channel as a mask. Select Create From Mask in the Objects menu to create an object out of the masked area. Now you can utilize Corel Photo–Paint's object-oriented approach to position the button over any background. This technique would be useful for creating buttons for multimedia.

Any number of buttons can be created with this technique. This variation was created by vertically condensing the circle, then changing the directions of the Linear Fountain Fills.

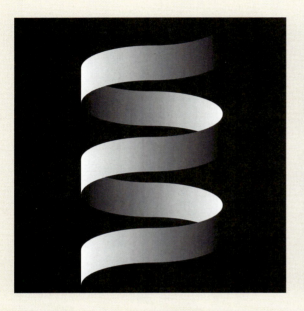

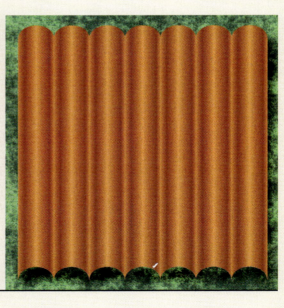

VARIATIONS

CorelDRAW's custom masks can create a multitude of special effects utilizing this technique. For example, the spirals from Project 2 and the corrugated extrusions from Project 5 were used to create these images.

26

Building Custom Borders with CorelDRAW and Corel Photo-Paint

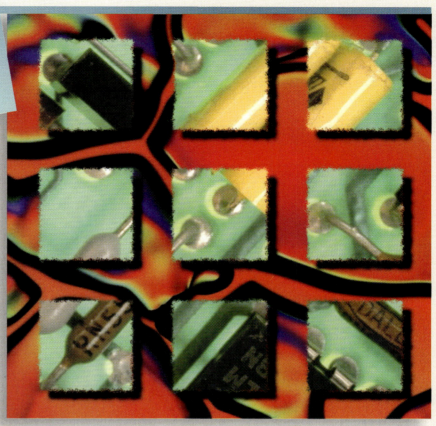

What you will learn

- Creating custom borders
- Working with clipping paths

B Bitmap images are mapped to a square or rectangle, which often results in bitmaps being printed or displayed as boring squares or rectangles. However, you can lose the squares and rectangles with clipping paths and a little creativity.

IMPORTANT NOTE: Although Corel Photo-Paint became available in CorelDRAW 3, Objects, Merge Modes, and Clipping Paths were introduced in Corel Photo-Paint 5, and the Alchemy effect was introduced in Corel Photo-Paint 5 Plus.

Creating Custom Borders

1 Begin in CorelDRAW by centering a 2.3-inch black square within a 2.5-inch white square. Make sure the black square is in front of the white square. Remove the outline. (The outline on the 2.5-inch square here is for illustration purposes only.) Save the file as BORDER1.CDR.

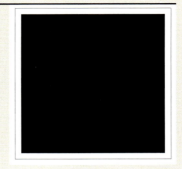

2 Open Corel Photo-Paint. Create a new image that is 2.5 inches square at your preferred resolution. Fill the document with any image. This example was created with Paul Gaugin's "Flowers" from the Masters III Corel Professional Photos CD-ROM collection. The tile background was resampled and cropped to 2.5 inches square. Once you have an image, save it as BORDER2.TIF. Close the file.

3 Open Border1.CDR in Corel Photo-Paint at your preferred resolution in RGB (16 million colors). The RGB color model is important because the effect that will be used in the next step works only in RGB mode.

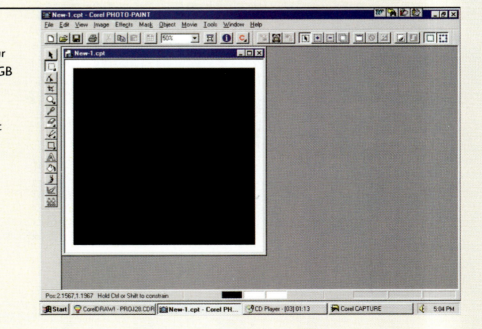

4 Select the Alchemy effect from Effects ➢ Artistic. Click on the Load button. The Load Brush dialog box should default to the Corel6\photopnt\ plgbrush directory. If not, change it. Select STDGRAD.BMP. Press OK. From Saved Styles library, select Style, then select Spatula. Click OK. Save the file as BORDER3.TIF.

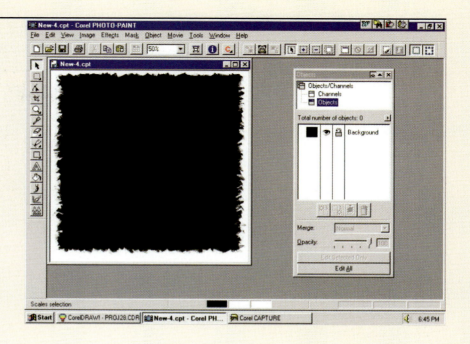

HINT

While this example uses a brush with a gradient blend in it, the effect shows up a little better with brushes that don't have gradations in them. You can create your own brushes for the Alchemy effect filter with CorelDRAW. Draw a box that is .42667 inches square. Create any image you wish within the box, then export it to the Corel6\photopnt\plgbrush directory as a Grayscale at 300 dpi Windows BMP. You can open any of the BMP files located in the directory in Corel Photo–Paint or CorelDRAW to get some ideas. Any brush can be used with the technique.

5 Select Paste From File from the Edit menu. Load the BORDER2.TIF file as an object. The black square to which you've applied the Alchemy filter should be the background, and the BORDER2.TIF file should be an object directly over the background. Sometimes objects do not get pasted directly in the center of the file. Open the Tool Settings Roll-Up (Ctrl+F8) with the object selected, and click on the Object Position tab. Enter 0 in both the horizontal and vertical settings. Leave the Relative position option unchecked. Press Apply. Open the Objects Roll-Up (Ctrl+F7). Select the Merge: Add mode. From Objects ➢ Combine, select Objects With Background. Save the file with a new name so that you do not overwrite BORDER3.TIF.

HINT Using this technique, any number of variations of the border can be created with the Alchemy filter. The values used in this example are not the only possible settings. Note, however, that the following settings cannot change: On the Brush tab, Layering must be set to Ordered. On the Alchemy filter's Color tab, Brush color must be Solid color (with Solid color set to Black); and Hue, Saturation, and Brightness should be set to 0. On the Angle tab, the "This:" setting should be set to -180, "That:" to 180; and Variation: 0. (These settings can actually change, but they provide for the maximum randomness.) On the Trans tab, the Vary brush transparency should be set to No Variation, and both the Transparency and Variation options must be set to 0.

Certain settings can be altered to produce a variety of variations. On the Size tab, the Vary brush size option can be set to either Randomly or By Brightness. The This/That options tend to work best at 5 and 30, respectively; but you can change them to vary the sizes of the brush. The Variation option can be altered, but 0 is recommended.

Working with Clipping Paths

1 If you need to use images in a layout, you will likely want to exclude the surrounding white background. To do this, load the BORDER2.TIF file as a channel, and load the channel as a mask. Select Invert from the Mask menu. Then, save the file as an Encapsulated PostScript (EPS) file. Corel Photo-Paint uses the mask information to create a clipping path. When the file is subsequently imported into CorelDRAW or a layout program such as Adobe PageMaker, the white areas will not print.

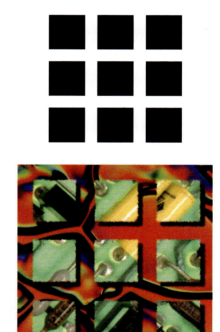

2 Of course, you are not limited to simple square shapes from CorelDRAW. There are plenty of other possibilities. For example, a diagonal shape from CorelDRAW can create a torn paper effect, multiple shapes can be used, and of course this technique can also work with text.

You do not have to create your borders with the Alchemy effect. These borders were created in CorelDRAW and were used as borders for imagery in Corel Photo-Paint without using the Alchemy effect. All of the photos in these examples are from Corel's Professional Photos CD-ROM collections.

27

Mastering Text Effects with CorelDRAW and Corel Photo-Paint

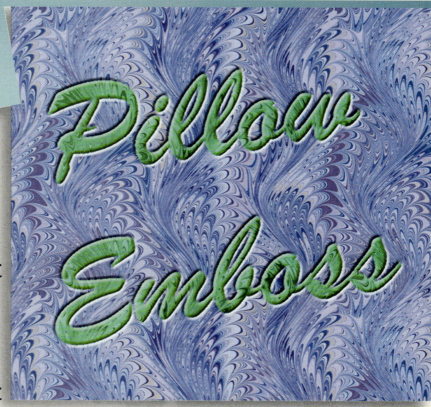

What you will learn

- Creating the pillow emboss or emboss effect
- Creating outer and inner glows
- Creating drop shadows

Even with editable text and the object-oriented approach provided by Corel Photo-Paint 6, using CorelDRAW to create the masks and layout can often be faster, easier, and more powerful. Also, masks created in CorelDRAW usually have much smaller file sizes than do masks created in Corel Photo-Paint.

IMPORTANT NOTE: Although Corel Photo-Paint became available in CorelDRAW 3, Objects, Merge Modes, and Clipping Paths were introduced in Corel Photo-Paint 5, and the Alchemy effect was introduced in Corel Photo-Paint 5 Plus.

Creating the Pillow Emboss or Emboss Effect

1 Begin in CorelDRAW by drawing a 2.5-inch black square. Type in some text (or position some shapes or clipart), fill with White, and assign no outline. This example utilizes CorelDRAW's handy alignment tools to center the text within the square, but you can position the text or clipart wherever you wish. Save the file. Close CorelDRAW.

2 Open Corel Photo-Paint. Open the pillow emboss mask you just created in CorelDRAW in your preferred resolution in grayscale (256 shades of gray). Select Gaussian Blur from Effects ➤ Blur. At 300 dpi, apply the Gaussian Blur effect with a radius setting of 5. Use a smaller radius setting with smaller dpi.

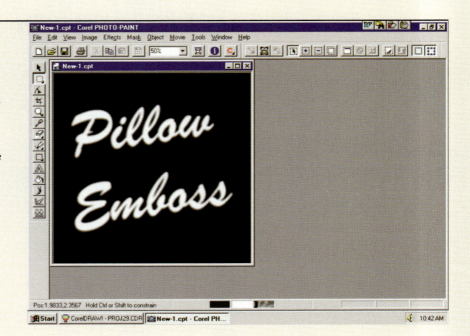

HINT

The Gaussian Blur effect is resolution dependent. The higher the resolution, the less the effect. For example, if a circle (example A) has the Gaussian Blur effect applied at a radius of 10 at 300 dpi, the result will be similar to example B. But if the same Gaussian Blur effect at radius 10 is applied to a circle at 72 dpi, the result will be similar to example C.

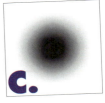

Introduced in Corel Photo-Paint 5 Plus, the Gaussian Blur effect was not shipped with the initial release of version 5. However, version 5 users can get the Gaussian Blur free with the latest revision of Corel Photo-Paint 5.

3 From Effects ➣ 3D Effects, select the Emboss effect. Apply the Emboss effect with a Gray Emboss color, Depth of 1, and an upper-left direction. Select Paste From File from the Edit menu. Paste the CorelDRAW pillow emboss mask as an object into Corel Photo-Paint. With the new object still selected, open the Tool Settings Roll-Up from View ➣ Roll-Ups. Change the horizontal and vertical settings of the Object Position tab to 0. Close the Tool Settings Roll-Up. Open the Objects Roll-Up. With the object still selected, select Logical XOR from the Merge drop-down list in the Objects Roll-Up (make sure Opacity is set to 100%). With the object still selected, select Objects With Background from Objects ➣

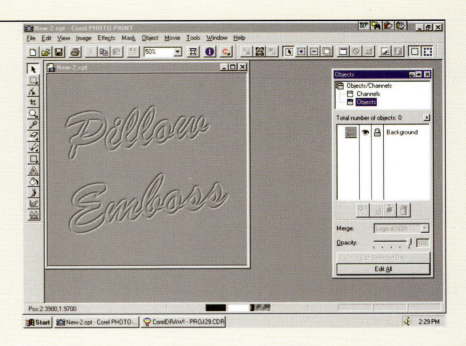

Combine. From Effects ➣ Blur, select the Soften effect. Apply it at 100%. Save the file.

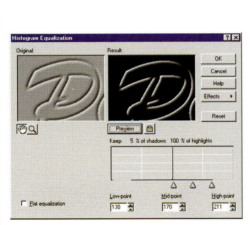

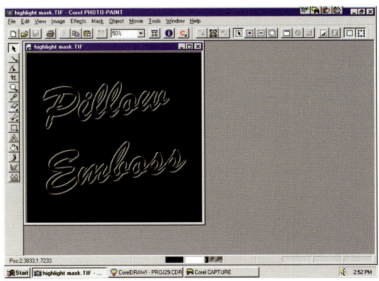

4 From Effects ➣ Color Adjust, select the Equalize effect. Turn off the Flat equalization option. Set the Low-point to 130, Mid-point to 170, and High-point to 211. Click OK. Select

Save As from the File menu, and save the file as HIGHLIGHT MASK.TIF or something similar. Select Undo from the Edit menu (or use the Undo List) to go back to the image before applying the Equalize effect. If you

cannot Undo to the point before the Equalize filter was applied, reopen the image you saved at the end of step 3.

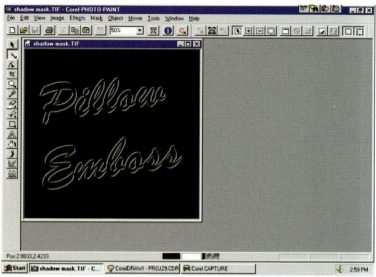

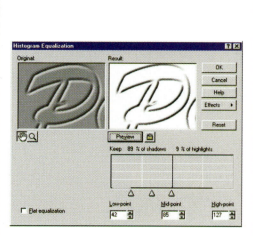

5 From Effects ➢ Color Adjust, select the Equalize effect. Turn off the Flat equalization option. Set the Low-point to 42, Mid-point to 85, and High-point to 127. Click OK. Select Save As from the File menu, and save the file as SHADOW MASK.TIF or something similar. Close the file.

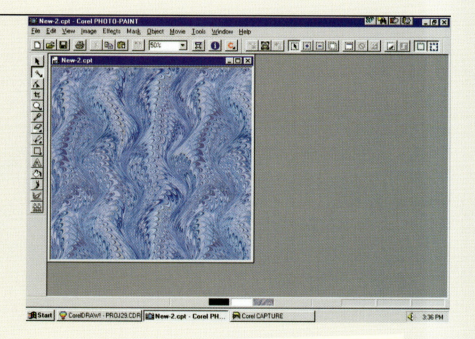

6 Open a new 2.5-inch-square file in Corel Photo-Paint at your preferred resolution. Fill the file with a seamless tile or cropped texture. This effect will work with most textures that provide enough contrast for the highlights and shadows of the effect. This texture was slightly altered from a seamless tile that comes with CorelDRAW 6. Corel Photo-Paint 5 Plus also comes with plenty of seamless tiles.

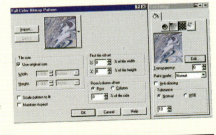

HINT

To fill a file with a seamless file, doubleclick on the Fill Tool on the Corel Photo-Paint toolbar. Click on the checkerboard button. Then, click on the Edit button to open the FullColor Bitmap Pattern dialog box. Click on the Import button, and locate the tile you wish to use. Click OK. Then, click anywhere within the file with the Fill Tool to fill the file with the tile.

7 Open the Channels Roll-Up. Load the HIGH-LIGHTS MASK file as a channel. Load the channel as a mask. Select Effects ➢ Color Adjust ➢ Brightness Contrast-Intensity. Apply the Brightness-Contrast-Intensity effect with a brightness of 100. Remove the mask. Delete the channel.

8 Load the SHADOW MASK file as a channel. Load the channel as a mask. Select Effects ➢ Color Adjust ➢ Brightness-Contrast-Intensity. Apply the Brightness-Contrast-Intensity effect with a brightness of 100. Remove the mask. Delete the channel.

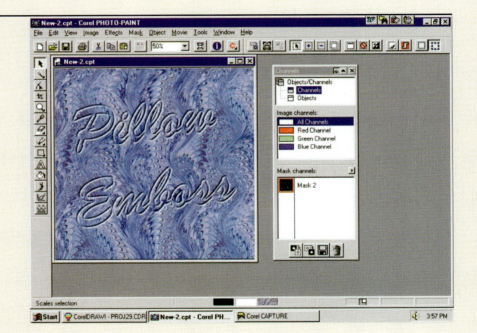

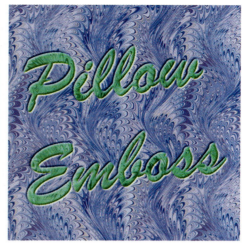

9 Load the original CorelDRAW file as a channel. Load the channel as a mask. At this point, you can do any number of things. You can adjust the Hue, Brightness, and so on. In this example, the Color Balance effect was utilized to create contrast between the text and the background.

HINT

Take a look at the differences between the file size of the original pillow emboss mask saved in CorelDRAW's format and the file size of the highlight and shadow masks created in Corel Photo-Paint. Even with compression, the highlight and shadow masks are more than 27 times as big. Ouch! This is one reason why it is usually better to create masks for Corel Photo-Paint whenever possible.

VARIATION

You can also use the original CorelDRAW mask to create an object out of the text area. When this object is placed upon a different background, a variant emboss effect results.

As mentioned earlier, text need not be the only source for masks to create the pillow emboss effect. This elevator button was created from a simple circle and an arrow from CorelDRAW's symbols using the pillow emboss technique.

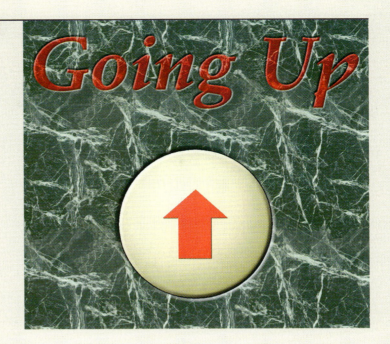

Creating Outer Glows

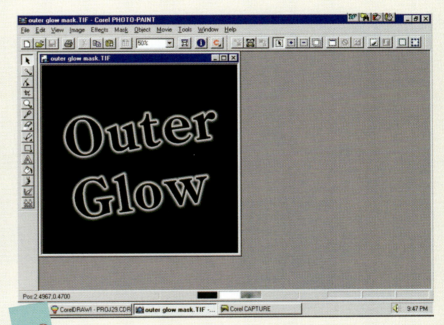

1 Begin in CorelDRAW by drawing a 2.5-inch black square. Type in some text (or position some shapes or clipart), fill with White, and assign no outline. Save the file. Close CorelDRAW.

2 Open Corel Photo-Paint. Create a new 2.5-inch-square white file at your preferred resolution. Open the Channels Roll-Up. Load the outer glow CorelDRAW file as a channel. Load the channel as a mask. Select Feather from the Mask menu. Apply a feather to the mask with the following settings: Width: 15; Direction: Outside; Edges: Hard. Select Invert from the Mask menu. Apply the Brightness-Contrast-Intensity effect with a brightness of -100. Reload the outer glow channel as a mask. Press Ctrl+F to apply the Brightness-Contrast-Intensity effect at -100 brightness again. Remove the mask and the channel. From the Blur menu, apply the Soften filter at 100%. Save the file as OUTER GLOW MASK.TIF. Close the file.

3 Create a new 2.5-inch–square file at the same resolution. Fill it with a seamless tile or a cropped background. This background was created from a seamless tile that comes with CorelDRAW 6. Open the Channels Roll-Up. Load OUTER GLOW MASK as a channel. Load the channel as a mask. Doubleclick on the Fill Tool. Click on the color wheel button in the Tool Settings Roll-Up. Click on the Edit button, and change the fill to solid yellow. Click on the rectangle tool. Draw a rectangle over the entire file. Remove the mask and the channel.

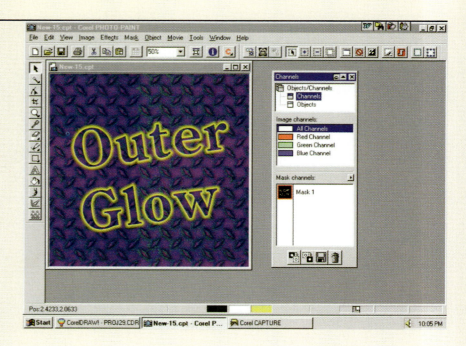

4 Load the outer glow CorelDRAW file as a channel. Load the channel as a mask. Change the fill to a different fill using another solid color, seamless tile, or texture fill. Click on the rectangle tool. Draw a rectangle over the entire file. Remove the mask and the channel.

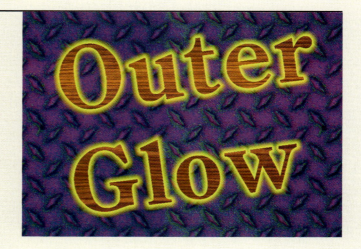

Creating Inner Glows

1 To create the inner glow, begin in CorelDRAW by drawing a 2.5-inch black square. Type in some text (or position some shapes or clipart), fill with White, and assign no outline. Save the file. Close CorelDRAW.

2 Open Corel Photo-Paint. Create a new 2.5-inch-square white file at your preferred resolution. Open the Channels Roll-Up. Load the inner glow CorelDRAW file as a channel. Load the channel as a mask. Select Feather from the Mask menu. Apply a feather to the mask with the following settings: Width: 15; Direction: Inside; Edges: Hard. Apply the Brightness-Contrast-Intensity effect with a brightness of -100. Reload the outer glow channel as a mask. Invert the mask. Press Ctrl+F to apply the Brightness-Contrast-Intensity effect at -100 brightness again. Remove the mask and the channel. Apply the Soften filter at 100%. Save the file as INNER GLOW MASK.TIF. Close the file.

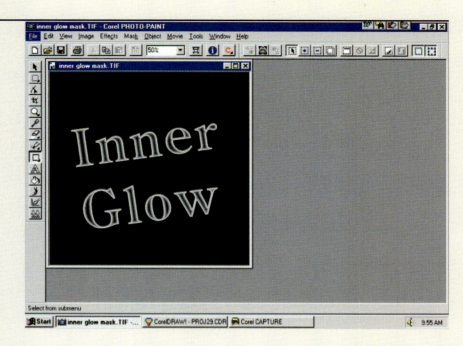

3 Create a new 2.5-inch-square file at the same resolution. Fill it with a seamless tile or a cropped background. This background was created from a seamless tile that comes with CorelDRAW 6. Open the Channels Roll-Up. Load INNER GLOW MASK as a channel. Load the channel as a mask. Double-click on the Fill Tool. Click on the color wheel button in the Tool Settings Roll-Up. Click on the Edit button, and change the fill to solid yellow. Click on the rectangle tool. Draw a rectangle over the entire file. Remove the mask and the channel.

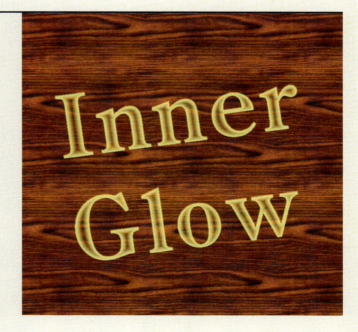

Creating Drop Shadows

1 Drop shadows are easier to create from within Corel Photo-Paint. Create a 2.5-inch-square file at your preferred resolution in Corel Photo-Paint. Fill it with a seamless tile or a cropped background. This background was created from a seamless tile that comes with CorelDRAW 6. Double-click on the Text Tool, and type in some text. After positioning your text, select Duplicate from the Object menu. Open the Objects Roll-Up. Close the Tool Settings Roll-Up.

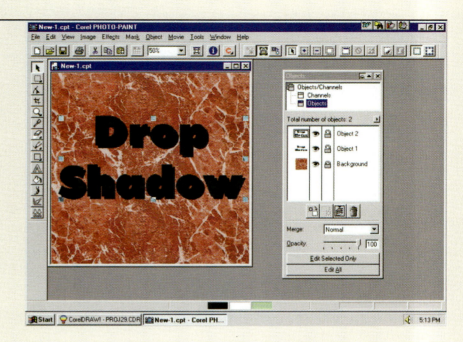

2 Click on the "eye" image in the Objects Roll-Up for the background, and duplicate object to hide them. Select the remaining object. Then, select Feather from the Object menu. Apply a feather with the settings as follows: Width: 10; Edges: Hard.

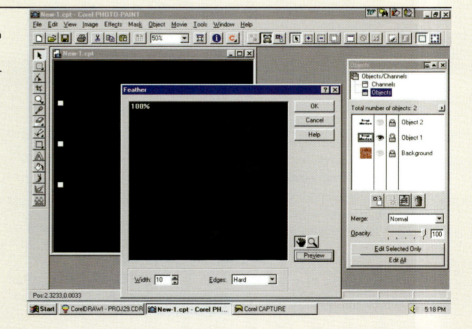

3 Click on the "eye" image in the Objects Roll-Up duplicate object to reveal it. Click on the "eye" image in the Objects Roll-Up original object to hide it. Fill the object with another color or texture by selecting the color or texture and drawing a rectangle that covers the whole object. Reposition the objects as you like, then combine them with the background.

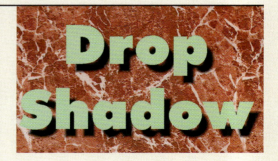

Appendix A

COMPARISON OF FEATURES IN CORELDRAW AND PHOTO-PAINT VERSIONS

Table A-1: Missing or Moved Features in CorelDRAW

Version 6 Feature	Version 6 Location	Version 5 Location/Equivalent	Version 4 Location/Equivalent
Wireframe	View	View	Display ➢ Edit Wireframe
Intersection	Arrange	Arrange ➢ Intersection	N/A
Trim	Arrange	Arrange ➢ Trim	N/A
PowerClip	Effects	Effects ➢ PowerClip	N/A
Automatically center new powerclip contents	Tools ➢ Options	Special ➢ Preferences ➢ Auto-Center Place Inside	N/A
Nudge	Tools ➢ Options	Special ➢ Preferences	Special ➢ Preferences
Place duplicates and clones	Tools ➢ Options	Special ➢ Preferences ➢ Place duplicates and clones	Special ➢ Preferences
Pattern	Tools ➢ Create	Special ➢ Create Pattern	Special ➢ Create Pattern
Lens	Effects	Effects ➢ Lens Roll-Up	N/A
Custom Fountain Fill	Tool Box ➢ Fill Tool ➢ Fountain Fill dialog	Tool Box ➢ Fill Tool ➢ Fountain Fill dialog	Tool Box ➢ Fill Tool ➢ Fountain Fill dialog ➢ Options
Join With Segment/Extend Curve to Close	Node Edit Roll-Up	N/A	N/A
Knife Tool	Tool Box ➢	N/A	N/A
Polygon Tool	Tool Box ➢	N/A	N/A
Position	Arrange ➢ Transform	Effects ➢ Transform Roll-Up	Arrange ➢ Move
Rotate	Arrange ➢ Transform	Effects ➢ Transform Roll-Up	Effects ➢ Rotate & Skew
Scale and Mirror	Arrange ➢ Transform	Effects ➢ Transform Roll-Up	Effects ➢ Stretch & Mirror...
Size	Arrange ➢ Transform	Effects ➢ Transform Roll-Up	N/A
Skew	Arrange ➢ Transform	Effects ➢ Transform Roll-Up	Effects ➢ Rotate & Skew

Table A-2: Table of Missing or Moved Features in Corel Photo-Paint

Version 6 Feature	Version 6 Location	Version 5 Location/Equivalent
Combine Objects with Background	Objects ➢ Combine ➢ Objects With Background	Objects ➢ Merge
Channels (Alpha Channels)	Channels Roll-Up	Mask , Transparency Mask
Brightness-Contrast-Intensity Effect	Effects ➢ Color Adjust ➢ Brightness-Intensity	Effects ➢ Color ➢ Brightness and Contrast
Equalize Effect	Effects ➢ Color Adjust ➢ Equalize	Effects ➢ Tone ➢ Equalize
Map to Object Effect	Effects ➢ 3D Effects ➢ Map to Object	Effects ➢ Mapping ➢ Map to Sphere
Soften Effect	Effects ➢ Blur ➢ Soften	Effects ➢ Soften ➢ Soften

Appendix B

GLOSSARY OF TERMS

Beziér—A method CorelDRAW uses to create curved surfaces. A Beziér curve has two endpoints and a set of control points that allow you to manipulate the shape of the curve.

Control points—Points extending from nodes along a curved object or curved line that control the angle at which the curve passes through the node. Control points only appear when you select a node or segment with the Shape Tool. Nodes on straight lines do not have control points.

CDR—CorelDRAW's file format.

Channels—Masks in Corel Photo-Paint used to create transparency effects.

Conical Fill—A type of fill that applies a gradient in a clockwise or counterclockwise direction.

Cusp—A type of node that allows a line to pass through it at a sharp angle. Node types can be assigned from the Node Edit Roll-Up.

DPI—Dots per inch.

Fountain Fill—A type of fill that applies a gradient from one or more colors to an object.

Group—A group collects objects and lines into a single selectable and manipulatable entity.

Guidelines—Nonprinting dashed lines used to align and position objects. The default color for guidelines is blue.

LPI—Lines per inch.

Marquee—The blue-dashed box seen when dragging around objects with the Pick Tool or nodes with the Shape Tool. Surrounding objects and nodes with a marquee box selects them.

Nodes—Small hollow squares along the outlines of objects and lines where two line segments meet. Nodes are used to manipulate the paths of a line segment. There are three types of nodes: cusp, smooth, and symmetrical.

TIF—Tagged image file format.

Tint—A percentage of a given color. For example, 30% Blue is a tint of Blue.

RESOURCES

Corel Corporation
1600 Carling Avenue
Ottawa, Canada K1Z 8R7
613-728-0826

Image Club
729 24th Avenue, S.E.
Calgary, Alberta, Canada T2G 5K8
403-262-8008

MetaTools
6303 Carpinteria Street
Carpinteria, CA 93013
805-566-6200

PhotoDisc, Inc.
2013 Fourth Avenue
Seattle, WA 98121
206-441-9355

Index